THE BREAKFAST BOOK
Recipes for the best meal of the day

Diana Troy

THE BREAKFAST BOOK

Illustrated by
BELINDA MURPHY

ALLISON & BUSBY
LONDON · NEW YORK

First published in Great Britain by
Allison and Busby Limited,
6a Noel Street, London WIV 3RB
and distributed in the USA by
Schocken Books Inc.
62 Cooper Square New York, NY 10003

British Library Cataloguing in Publication Data:
Troy, Diana
  The breakfast book
  1. Breakfasts
  I. Title
641.5′2   TX733

ISBN 0–85031–623–5

Phototypeset by Falcon Graphic Art Ltd
Wallington, Surrey
Printed in Great Britain by
Mackays of Chatham Ltd

Contents

Acknowledgements

Welsh Oatcakes — *Taste of Wales*, Theodora FitzGibbon: J.M. Dent, 1971

Flummery — *Food in England*, Dorothy Hartley: Macdonald, 1954

Strawberry Fritters — *Fruit Book*, Jane Grigson: Michael Joseph, 1982

Hamine Eggs — *A Book of Middle Eastern Food*, Claudia Roden: Thomas Nelson, 1968

Mushroom Omelette — *French Provincial Cooking*, Elizabeth David: Michael Joseph, 1977

Kidneys — *Taste of Ireland*, Theodora FitzGibbon: J.M. Dent, 1968

Worcester Sauce — *Jams, Pickles and Chutneys*, D & R Mabey: Penguin, 1976

Cods' Roe Recipe — *Taste of Ireland*, Theodora FitzGibbon: J.M. Dent, 1968

Tangerine Jam — *A Book of Middle Eastern Food*, Claudia Roden: Thomas Nelson, 1968

Cumberland Sausages — *The Farmhouse Kitchen*, Mary Norwak: Ward Lock, 1975

To my grandmother, Annie Harvey

Thanks to everyone who suggested and tried recipes.

Many thanks to my mother who laboriously typed out the manuscript, and to Tansy who was enthusiastic about the whole thing.

"Take a good meal at morn,
unknown it is where at eve you may be"

Introduction

Breakfast is a meal in limbo. Most people would agree that it is a necessary meal, most people eat it, at least sometimes. Nutritionists assure us that it is the most important meal of the day, yet hardly anyone reckons to spend any time or imagination either on its contents or its presentation. Looking through well-stocked cookery shelves in bookshops and libraries, one searches almost in vain for any mention of breakfast. Hoping for some interesting and exotic ideas on the subject, I wrote to some well-known hotels and asked them to send me their breakfast menus. But even they had little to suggest apart from the usual cornflakes, bacon and egg, rolls and croissants.

Perhaps our breakfasts are usually so boring and stereotyped because most of us get up so late. Perhaps we are all too benumbed and bleary-eyed to actually choose food first thing in the morning. In this zombie-like state, we can do no more than obey the advertisers' instructions to "Go to work on an egg" or "Start the day the Kellogg's way". Perhaps the advertisers have it all their own way, working on our unresisting early-morning subconscious. On reflection, the most notable breakfasts I can remember (on a farm or kibbutz, for example) have been eaten after some hours of outdoor work. Puritanical though it may sound, breakfast always seems to go down better after one has literally worked up an appetite.

Breakfast has had a mixed history in this country over the last few hundred years. In the Middle Ages, many people went to Mass in the morning and "dined" early (the dining hour became progressively later with each century). Since people could not eat before going to Mass, and by the time they came back, dinner time was already approaching, breakfast was no more than a light snack. The labouring poor no doubt had a ladle of pottage and a drink of ale — much the same as they ate and drank for their other meals. By the eighteenth century, however, breakfast had become a social occasion among the upper classes: Goldsmith wrote that "People of fashion make public breakfasts at the Assembly Houses". Their breakfast would have consisted of coffee and chocolate (both recently introduced into Europe), little cakes called "wigs" and, no doubt, plenty of urbane conversation. A hundred years later, Victorian respectability had taken over, breakfast had become part of the domestic ritual in well-heeled families. There were plenty of servants in these households, to get up early and prepare the lavish and complicated dishes which Mrs Beeton so often recommends. Many people still worked on the land, of course, and in farmhouses up and down the country, huge breakfasts were prepared to sustain the workers through the morning. Not a few recipes in this book originated in the farmhouses of England, Scotland, Wales and Ireland.

In these days, late risers, urban dwellers, servantless though most of us are, is it possible for there to be any revival of "the comfortable meal called breakfast", as Mrs Beeton calls it? Surely it is worth a try. After all, we do not have to get up and light the fire before we can begin to prepare our breakfasts, as our ancestors had to. We also have access to a wider range of foodstuffs and culinary ideas from all over the world than ever before. (In this book I have tried to collect breakfast ideas from as many countries as possible.)

With time, or lack of it, in mind, I have tried in this book to include a lot of breakfasts which do not take long to prepare. Some recipes can be mixed up in the evening and left overnight to rise, soak or stand and quickly cooked in the morning. Others can be prepared in advance — fruit and dairy recipes, for example — and stored in the refrigerator. Quite a few recipes involve baking which, since home-baked products always keep so well, can be done at a convenient moment and eaten over the course of several days. Some recipes use up cooked foods, like potatoes or rice, which have been left over from the previous day. If I have included some recipes which seem rather time-consuming, it is because they seemed too interesting to omit. Such recipes may perhaps be saved for special occasions (or merely savoured in the imagination).

Those who remain unconvinced of the benefits and pleasures of early-morning breakfast may always enjoy breakfast at some other time of day. They may even like to imitate and perversity of Lewis Carroll's Snark who "frequently breakfasts at five o'clock tea and dines the following day"! Breakfast is too good a meal to miss out on altogether, so if it eludes you in the morning, try to catch up on it later in the day.

BREAD AND BUTTER

"Gentle Bakers! Bake good bread! For good bread doth comfort, confirm and doth establish a man's heart."

Andrew Borde

"The French people, as is well known, have the highest rate of bread consumption in Europe. No doubt this is why there is less illness in France."

Alexandre Dumas, *Grand Dictionnaire de cuisine*

Bread

For centuries, bakers have worked through the night so that people might enjoy the pleasures of freshly baked bread for breakfast. For bread is by far the most popular breakfast of the Western world, whether it is dipped in bowls of coffee as in France, eaten with cheese and sausage as in Germany, toasted with butter and marmalade as in England or dipped in olive oil, Mediterranean fashion.

Homer tells of Ulysses breakfasting at dawn on bread steeped in wine and bread was being cooked on flat, heated stones in Egypt from at least 3500 BC. The Egyptians made all the main technological breakthroughs, like the invention of the beehive oven and the discovery of the leavening process. Since then the techniques of breadmaking have only become more elaborate.

Wheat has always been the main flour used for bread-making, though rye and barley have also been widely used in areas where wheat does not easily grow. All through the Middle Ages in Europe, wheat flour was mixed with rye to make "maslin" — the bread of the common people for centuries. The rule of white bread for the rich and brown bread (brown because unrefined and/or mixed with rye flour) for the poor held good in England until the middle of the nineteenth century, when for the first time, white bread actually became cheaper than brown. Since that time (and before) the relative virtues of white bread and brown have been hotly debated with nutritionists often arguing in vain against the prejudice of centuries.

Not wishing to thrust my own preference for wholewheat flour too forcefully on the reader, I have given many recipes in which either type of flour may be used. I would not hesitate, however, to pass on my conviction that home-made bread is far superior to any which is commerically made, however good. No machine can really replace the process of hand kneading. It is a misconception that bread-making is a time-consuming occupation: as Elizabeth David says, it takes time, but not your time — the dough may need to be left some time to rise, but this does not require your active participation. With breakfast in mind, I have mentioned the possibility, in some recipes, of leaving the dough to rise overnight. In this way you can have fresh bread for breakfast without having to rise at dawn.

General Hints on Bread-making

1. The liquid measurements given in recipes are not an exact guide because different flours absorb differing amounts of water. With a little practice, one can tell by the feel of the dough how much liquid to use. The dough should be elastic and just wet enough to come away cleanly from the side of the mixing bowl.

2. Yeast may be used fresh or dried. Use double the amount of fresh yeast as dried. Dried yeast needs to have a little sugar or honey added to it to make it "work". Sprinkle the yeast into a small bowl of warm water and leave it for about five minutes, by which time it should have dissolved and formed a cushion of foam on the top of the liquid.

3. Yeasted bread should be made in warm conditions: a warm bowl, warm flour, warm water, all help the bread to rise. Try and leave the dough to rise in a place where there is a gentle all round heat. You can also place the bowl of rising dough inside a closed plastic bag. This is the best way to leave dough rising overnight so that it will not dry out.

4. When the bread is taken out of the oven, it should be taken out of the tin immediately and placed upside-down for the steam to escape. Leave it like this for a few hours and then store in a bread-tin or crock, i.e. a container which is not completely airtight. Earthenware crocks are ideal because, being unglazed, they are slightly porous; a metal bin with a small hole in the lid is also quite all right.

5. Wheatgerm, the heart of the wheat grain, improves the flavour, texture and nutritional value of wheat flour and a tablespoon to every pound of flour can always be added to advantage. (Hovis loaves were originally made from white flour with added wheatgerm.) Bran may also be added to improve the roughage content of the bread.

6. Always soak the mixing bowl as soon as the dough has been removed, otherwise it will be difficult to wash.

WHOLEWHEAT BREAD

1 kg (2 lb) wholewheat flour
125 g (4 oz) vegetable margarine
2 teaspoons salt
2 tablespoons black treacle or brown sugar
15 g (½ oz) dried yeast (or 30 g/1 oz fresh)
600 ml (1 pint) water

Mix the flour with the salt and cream the yeast with the treacle or sugar in a little of the warmed water. Rub the margarine into the flour then, when the yeast is creamed, add it to the flour mixture. Add the rest of the liquid slowly, mixing it in as you go along. Mix and knead for about 5 minutes, adding more water if the dough is too dry. Grease two 500 g (1 lb) size bread tins and divide the dough between the two tins. Leave in a warm place to rise until the dough comes nearly to the top of the tin. Wholewheat bread only needs to rise once. Preheat the oven to 400° F (200° C, Gas mark 6). Bake the loaves at this temperature for 15 minutes then at 375° F (190° C, Gas mark 5) for another 25–30 minutes. Test whether the loaves are done by inserting a knife blade into the middle of each: if this comes out clean, remove the bread from the tins and leave upside-down to cool.

WHITE BREAD

840 g (28 oz) plain white flour
120 g (4 oz) wheatgerm
15 g (½ oz) dried yeast (or 30 g/1 oz fresh)
2 teaspoons salt
600 ml (1 pint) water

Sift the flour with the salt and cream the yeast in a little of the warmed water. Add one teaspoon of sugar to the yeast if it is dried. Pour the creamed yeast into the flour and add the rest of the water. Mix the dough until all the water has been absorbed, then knead for a couple of minutes. Leave in a warm place to rise for 1½ to 2 hours or until the dough has about doubled its size. Knock down and knead again for about 5 minutes and place in two oiled 500 g (1 lb) bread tins. Leave to rise for a further 45 minutes, or until the bread is up to the top of the tins. Bake at just over 400° F (200° C, Gas mark 6) for the first 15 minutes and 375° F (190° C, Gas mark 5) for the remaining 30 minutes. Test with a knife blade and, if the bread is done, turn it out of the tins to cool.

An overnight rise enhances the flavour of white bread. After first mixing and kneading, cover the bowl containing the dough with polythene and leave to rise overnight. In the morning, knock down and knead again and leave for a short rise.

SOURDOUGH BREAD

For the leaven: 180 g (6 oz) wholewheat flour
1 tablespoon honey
400 ml (⅔ pint) water

For the bread: 1 kg (2 lb) wholewheat flour
1 teaspoon salt
2 tablespoons oil

Mix the flour, honey and water of the leavening mixture together in a jug and leave to stand at room temperature until it is quite fizzy (about three days). Then mix the dry flour and salt together in a bowl and add the leaven. Knead and put the dough in a warm place to rise (preferably overnight). When the dough has doubled in size, knock down and knead again and work in the oil. Put into two small or one large tin and leave to rise again. Bake for 15 minutes at 400° F (200° C, Gas mark 6) and a further 25 minutes at 375° F (190° C, Gas mark 5).

MILK BREAD

This bread has a soft crust and a sweet taste. Children seem to like it.

1 kg (2 lb) 85% flour, or 1 lb 10 oz wholewheat and 6 oz plain white
**   flour**
15 g (½ oz) dried yeast (or 30 g/1 oz fresh)
2 tablespoons treacle
60 g (2 oz) butter
2 teaspoons salt
600 ml (1 pint) milk

Mix the flour and salt. In a small amount of warm water, dissolve the yeast with the treacle if the yeast is dried (if not, add the treacle to the warm milk). Warm the milk and butter in a saucepan, then add first the yeast then the milk mixture gradually to the flour. Knead well and leave to rise in 1 kg (2 lb)-size bread tins until the dough has risen near the top of the tins. Bake at 400° F (200° C, Gas mark 6) for 15 minutes and 375° F (190° C, Gas mark 5) for a further 30 minutes.

POTATO BREAD

In earlier times when the wheat crop had to be eked out from harvest to harvest, vegetables such as parsnips, pumpkins and even ground up beans were often added to the wheat flour to make it go further.

Potatoes may also be added to wheat flour to make delicious light-textured bread, which is in no way inferior to pure wheat bread. Because it is quite moist, it keeps well for up to a week. The potatoes should be freshly cooked and not soggy. Cook them in their skins, drain them and let them dry off a little, then push them through a fine wire sieve. Elizabeth David specially recommends this bread for toasting and frying.

660 g (22 oz) 85% wholewheat flour or 540 g combined plain and wholewheat (18 oz wholewheat and 120 g (4 oz) plain flour)
300 g (10 oz) warm, milled potatoes
15 g (½ oz) dried (or 30 g/1 oz fresh) yeast
1 tablespoon salt
3 tablespoons olive oil or butter or margarine
1½ tablespoons brown sugar or treacle
600 ml (1 pint) warm water and milk, mixed

Sift the flour with the salt and add the warm sieved potatoes. Cream the yeast with the sugar or treacle and a little of the warmed water. Add the yeast and the rest of the liquid gradually to the flour and potato mixture. Mix well and add the oil or melted butter. Knead for a few minutes then leave to rise in a warm place for 1½–2 hours, or until the dough is doubled in size. Break down, knead and transfer to two 500 g (1 lb) size bread tins. Leave to rise for another half-hour or so, or until the dough has risen to near the top of the tins. Bake at 425° F (220° C, Gas mark 7) for about 10 minutes and 375° F (190°

17

C, Gas mark 5) for a further 35 minutes. This bread turns out well even if it is only given one rise.

Instead of potatoes, try also adding cooked rice or cooked buckwheat to this recipe.

RYE BREAD

As rye flour contains almost no gluten, pure rye bread, as eaten in parts of Germany, is extremely dense, dark-coloured and moist. It is generally cooked in special steam ovens for a very long time.

It is quite possible to make a good mixed wheat and rye loaf at home, however. Rye and wheat sourdough bread is popular in Eastern Europe but the preparation time for making this bread is quite lengthy. This recipe uses yeast and is relatively quick to make:

½ kg (1 lb) rye flour
½ kg (1 lb) wheatmeal flour (85%)
15 g (½ oz) dried yeast (or 1 oz fresh)
2 tablespoons black treacle
2 teaspoons salt
90 g (3 oz) caraway seeds (optional)
600 ml (1 pint) warm water

Mix the flours, salt and caraway seeds (saving some for the top of the loaves). Cream the yeast with the treacle in a little of the warmed water then, when it is ready, add to the flour. Add the rest of the

liquid by degrees, stirring. Be sure not to make this dough too wet. Knead and leave to rise for one to two hours, or until doubled in size. Knock down the dough and knead again, then put into two oiled 500 g (1 lb) tins and leave to rise for a further 45 minutes or so. Bake at 400° F (200° C, Gas mark 6) for the first 10 minutes, then at 375° F (190° C, Gas mark 5) for another 40–50 minutes (rather longer than usual).

SWEDISH RYE CRISPBREAD

In Scandinavia, biscuit-like breads, such as this one, are made in large, circular pieces with holes in the middle. They are stored in piles on an upright stick.

120 g (4 oz) rye flour
120 g (4 oz) wholewheat or plain flour
120 g (4 oz) vegetable margarine
1 teaspoon mixed herbs
½ teaspoon salt

Mix the flours and the salt and rub in the vegetable margarine. Add a little water to make a stiff dough. Roll out to a thickness of ¼-inch and cut into rectangles. Prick the biscuits all over with a fork and place on oiled baking trays. Pre-heat the oven to 375° F (190° C, Gas mark 5) and bake for 15 minutes or until slightly brown. Allow to cool thoroughly and store in an airtight tin.

THREE AMERICAN CORNBREADS

240 g (8 oz) cornmeal
300 g (10 oz) plain or 85% flour
2 level teaspoons baking powder
1 level teaspoon salt
60 g (2 oz) brown sugar
1 beaten egg
150 ml (¼ pint) yoghurt
2 tablespoons melted butter
150 ml (¼ pint) milk

19

Sift the dry ingredients together. Warm the milk and melt the butter in it. Beat the egg and add it to the dry ingredients. Stir in the yoghurt and then the milk and butter mixture until a fairly moist dough is obtained. Turn the mixture into a 1 kg (2 lb) bread tin and bake in a hot oven, 400° F (200° C, Gas mark 6), for 30 minutes.

240 g (8 oz) **fine cornmeal**
90 g (3 oz) **wholewheat flour**
1 teaspoon **salt**
1 teaspoon **baking powder**
90 g (3 oz) **butter**
60 g (2 oz) **brown sugar**
2 **eggs**
200 ml (⅓ pint) **boiling water**

Mix together the cornmeal, flour, baking powder, salt and sugar. Separate the two eggs and add the yolks to the flour mixture. Beat up the whites until they are stiff. Melt the butter in the boiling water and pour the liquid into the flour mixture. Stir very well and allow to cool for a couple of minutes. Then fold in the beaten egg whites and transfer the mixture immediately to a greased 500 g (1 lb) baking tin. Bake in a hot oven, 400° F (200° C, Gas mark 6), for half an hour.

SPOON BREAD

This speciality of the Southern States is really a kind of soufflé. It is easy to make but be sure to use very fine-ground yellow cornmeal (which can often be bought at Indian, if not wholefood, grocers). I found the original recipe rather bland so have invented my own. This should be served with something savoury, such as smoked fish or crisp bacon.

160 g (5½ oz) **fine yellow cornmeal**
450 ml (¾ pint) **water**
150 ml (¼ pint) **of milk**
4 **eggs**
2 tablespoons **butter**
1 teaspoon **salt**
2 heaped tablespoons **Parmesan cheese**
Black pepper
3 crushed cloves **garlic** (optional)

"Heat the oven to 400° F (200° C, Gas mark 6). Beat the eggs and keep them aside. Boil the water in a large saucepan and, while it is still boiling, add the cornmeal and the salt and pepper, stirring hard. Take off the heat. With an egg whisk, beat in the butter, milk, eggs, garlic and grated cheese until the mixture is of a smooth, batter-like consistency. Transfer to a greased soufflé or casserole dish and bake at 400° F (200° C, Gas mark 6) for 45 minutes.

SODA BREAD

Soda bread originated in relatively isolated regions of Wales and Ireland where ale yeast was unobtainable. The bread is leavened with buttermilk and bicarbonate of soda. As it rises in the baking, it is very quick to make. If the oven is turned on a little in advance, the whole process can be completed in half an hour, so it is possible to make soda bread in the morning for breakfast (it is very good hot from the oven).

This recipe makes one loaf:

½ kg (1 lb) wholewheat or plain flour
1 teaspoon salt
1 teaspoon bicarbonate of soda
200–300 ml (⅓–½ pint) buttermilk

Pre-heat the oven to 375° F (190° C, Gas mark 5). Sift the dry ingredients and add the liquid, mixing by hand until an even consistency is reached. The dough should be fairly stiff and it is not necessary to knead as with yeasted dough. Form the dough into a round loaf and incise a large cross on the top. Place on a greased baking tray and bake for 35 minutes. Test with the blade of a knife.

If it is not possible to obtain buttermilk, make up the liquid with half milk and half water and add two teaspoons of baking powder instead of bicarbonate of soda. Half yoghurt and half water also produces a good result.

BARLEY SODA BREAD

This is a delicious bread which goes especially well with savoury foods. It is sweet, close-textured and chewy and keeps well for days, if not weeks. (Barley has great keeping qualities.) In Norway, bread baked of pure barley meal kept so well that it was sometimes baked only twice a year and stored between whiles!

420 g (14 oz) wholewheat or plain flour
300 g (10 oz) barley meal
1½ teaspoons bicarbonate of soda
1½ teaspoons salt
300–400 ml (½–¾ pint) of buttermilk

The method is exactly the same as the recipe for soda bread, but form the dough into two loaves instead of one. It is best to cover the loaves with tin foil or an inverted cake tin for the first half of the baking time, otherwise the crust will be very hard.

POPPY SEED ROLLS

½ kg (1 lb) plain flour or plain and wholewheat mixed
1 teaspoon salt
1 teaspoon sugar
1 level teaspoon dried yeast (2 teaspoons fresh)
120 g (4 oz) butter
300 ml (½ pint) milk and water mixed

Dissolve the yeast in a little of the warmed water with the sugar. Sift the flour and salt. Mix in the yeast and the rest of the liquid, stirring. Knead the dough (it should not be too moist because the butter is still to be added). Leave in a warm place for at least half an hour or until the dough has doubled in size. Soften, but not melt, the butter and work it into the risen dough by hand. Divide into about a dozen rolls and put them on a greased baking tray to rise again — for about 20 minutes. Pre-heat the oven to 400° F (200° C, Gas mark 6). Bake the rolls at this temperature for 10 minutes then take them out of the oven, brush with a little milk and sprinkle with poppy seeds. Lower the oven temperature to 375° F (190° C, Gas mark 5) and bake for a further 10 minutes.

BAPS (SCOTTISH BREAKFAST ROLLS)

This is a very successful recipe for rolls. Traditionally, baps are made with plain white flour, but I think it is an improvement to add some wheatgerm to the flour. Instead of the lard which is usual in this recipe, you can use vegetable margarine or butter. It is important to knead rolls well for the second time as this helps them to keep their shape. This recipe makes about a dozen rolls.

390 g (13 oz) plain flour
90 g (3 oz) wheatgerm
1 teaspoon salt
90 g (3 oz) lard, margarine or butter
15 g (½ oz) brown sugar
15 g (½ oz) dried yeast (or 30 g/1 oz fresh)
300 ml (½ pint) milk and water mixed

Cream the yeast with the sugar in a little of the warmed water. Sift the dry ingredients and rub in the fat. Add the creamed yeast and the rest of the warmed liquid gradually to the flour, stirring all the time. Knead well and leave the dough to rise in a covered bowl for ½–1hr to one hour. Knock down the dough and knead again. Shape into rolls. Leave again to rise, this time as little as 20 minutes may be enough. Pre-heat the oven to 400° F (200° C, Gas mark 6). Just before putting the rolls in the oven, brush them with water and dust them with flour. Bake for 10 minutes at 400° F (200° C, Gas mark 6) and a further 10 minutes at 375° F (190° C, Gas mark 5).

In this recipe and the previous one, the dough may be mixed up and left to rise overnight. In the morning, the rest of the preparation can be carried out quite quickly and the rolls can be eaten hot from the oven.

QUICK BREAKFAST ROLLS

These rolls are more like scones than yeasted rolls, as they are leavened with bicarbonate of soda. They are very good eaten straight from the oven.

480 g (1 lb) plain flour or 85% wholewheat flour
90 g (3 oz) butter or margarine
1 teaspoon salt
2 level teaspoons bicarbonate of soda
1 egg
300 ml (½ pint) of milk

Pre-heat the oven to 375° F (190° C, Gas mark 5). Mix the dry ingredients and rub in the butter. Add the milk and the beaten egg. The mixture should be soft but not runny. Divide into about twelve rolls and place them on a greased baking tray. Incise a cross on top of each one to prevent cracking. Bake for 25 minutes.

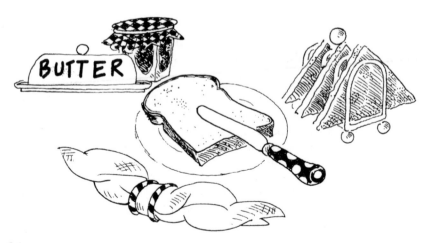

TOAST

Buttered toast, as Elizabeth David points out, is an English speciality. It is recorded in history and alluded to in literature. In the Middle Ages, pieces of bread were dipped in wine, then retoasted to be spread with thick pastes of quinces, raisins, spices and sugar. (In the seventeenth century a paste of cinnamon, sugar and wine, went to America with the Pilgrim Fathers, where it survived and gathered popularity as "cinnamon toast".) In Victorian and Edwardian times, savouries were relished on toast. George Eliot in *The Mill on the Floss* recalls the "smell of hot toast and ale from the kitchen at the breakfast hour".

Many kinds of bread can be used for toast, from light airy white loaves to solid wholewheat bread. Soda bread and potato bread make very good toast. Elizabeth David recommends making toast, if you are not lucky enough to have an open fire, on a ridged metal plate placed over a gas flame or an electric plate. Making toast under a grill is perfectly all right, except for the totally absent-minded who may have to resort to an automatic toaster.

Stale bread can receive a new lease of life by being dipped in cold water for a few seconds, then put it in a hot oven for five to ten minutes.

CROISSANTS

Croissants did not originate in France as one might expect, but in Budapest in the seventeenth century. The Turks had laid seige to Budapest and had even constructed tunnels under the city, by which they hoped to enter unobserved. Bakers working during the night, however, heard their movements and foiled their plan. In commemoration of this notable service to the city, the bakers invented a special rich type of bread and baked it in the shape of the infamous Turkish crescent. Little did they realize how popular their invention would prove.

This recipe make about two dozen croissants. It is worth making a good amount of dough at a time as the whole process is quite laborious and, once the mixing is done, it can be left in the refrigerator until required.

600 g (20 oz) plain white flour
300 g (10 oz) butter
15 g (½ oz) dried yeast (30 g/1 oz fresh)
2 level teaspoons salt
30 g (1 oz) sugar
200 ml (¼ pint) milk and a small amount of water

Cream the yeast with the sugar in a small cup of warm water. Bring the milk to the boil, then pour it into a basin with 30 g (1 oz) of the butter. Allow to cool a little then add the dissolved yeast and the flour. Knead well together to make a fairly firm dough. Leave to rise in a warm place until doubled in size. Knead for a few minutes, then leave the dough to chill for 1½–2 hours. Take it out of the refrigerator and roll out into an oblong piece. Spread the rest of the butter evenly over the surface of the dough, then fold in each end of the strip. Give it a half turn and roll across the join. Chill in the fridge for another half-hour, then repeat the rolling and turning process twice to ensure that the butter is evenly distributed. The dough may then be left in the refrigerator overnight or for at least another hour. After this time, take out as much dough as required and roll it out to a thickness of ¼". Cut into squares of about 5 inches and cut these into triangles. Roll each triangle starting with the long edge and finishing with the point and bend the ends round to form crescents. Arrange on an ungreased baking tray and allow to rise at warm room temperature for about an hour. Bake for about 20 minutes at 375° F (190° C, Gas mark 5).

Just before baking, you can brush the croissants with a glaze made from one egg yolk and two tablespoons of milk, but this is not essential.

BRIOCHE

This recipe is not difficult but it involves rather more time for the rising of the dough, so plan it a day ahead. The result is worth waiting for.

240 g (8 oz) plain flour
1 teaspoon dried yeast (2 teaspoons fresh)
120 g (4 oz) unsalted butter
2 eggs
1 level teaspoon salt
1 tablespoon sugar
A little warm milk

Sift the flour and salt. Cream the yeast in a little warm water, with the sugar if the yeast is dried, or in a little warm milk if it is fresh; when it is ready, add it to the flour, then mix in the previously beaten eggs. Have ready 120 g (4 oz) of very soft but not melted butter and work it into the dough by hand. The dough should be consistent and fairly moist at this stage; if it seems too dry, add in a little more milk. Leave to rise in a warm place for 2–3 hours, by which time it should be doubled or more in size. Break down the dough and then leave in an unheated, but not too cold place overnight, or for several hours. When it is again well risen, knead it for a few minutes and transfer to a well greased tin — either a small cake tin or the traditional fluted brioche mould. Leave again for 2–3 hours, this time in a warm place until the dough is up to the top of the mould, then bake at 400° F (200° C, Gas mark 6) for 25–30 minutes. Turn out and allow to cool. The loaf may be glazed in the same way as a Sally Lunn. Brioche and fresh fruit makes a light and delicious breakfast.

MUFFINS

In Victorian times, muffins were part of the breakfast ritual. They were generally bought, rather than made at home, from the muffin men who did their rounds each morning. They were kept hot in a napkin by the fire until breakfast time. If too much time elapsed between the buying and the eating, they were toasted on the outsides and then split and buttered. This recipe is not at all difficult or time-consuming, since the muffins are left to rise overnight. It is a treat to have muffins hot from the oven for breakfast.

½ kg (1 lb) flour (either all plain or ⅔ plain and ⅓ brown)
1 level teaspoon salt
8 g (¼ oz) dried yeast (or ½ oz fresh)
30 g (1 oz) sugar
90 g (3 oz) butter
1 egg
Milk to mix (about 200 ml/⅓ pint)

Sift the flour and salt and cream the yeast in a little warm milk, if it is fresh, in a little warm water with the sugar if it is dried. Melt the butter and mix it into the flour with the yeast. Add the beaten egg and enough warm milk to make a rather liquid dough. Mix all the ingredients well together and leave the bowl, covered with polythene, at normal room temperature overnight. In the morning turn out the dough on to a well floured board (it should be just dry enough to be able to do this, but still moist and springy), press it out with the palm of the hand to a thickness of about one inch and cut into circles with a glass. Leave in a warm place to double in size, which will take between 20–30 minutes. Pre-heat the oven to 425° F (220° C, Gas mark 7) and bake the muffins on an oiled tray for about 15 minutes. The muffins should have a thin crisp crust and a very soft, light inside. Split and butter the muffins and eat them while they are still warm.

AMERICAN MUFFINS

American muffins are more quickly made than the English ones, since they are mixed with baking powder rather than yeast. They are cooked in special tins with large shallow pans. They should be mixed very lightly, just enough to wet the dry ingredients.

150 g (5 oz) wholewheat flour
150 g (5 oz) plain flour
60 g (2 oz) melted butter
60 g (2 oz) sugar
1 egg
½ teaspoon salt
2 level teaspoons baking powder
A little under ½ pint (300 ml) milk

Pre-heat the oven to 375° F (190° C, Gas mark 5), sift the dry ingredients. In a saucepan melt the butter, then stir in the milk. Beat in the egg. Stir these liquid ingredients into the dry and mix very lightly. These muffins should double in size when cooked, so fill the muffin tins accordingly. Bake for 25 minutes.

For cornmeal or bran muffins, substitute one-third of the flour in the above recipe for cornmeal or bran respectively.

For bacon muffins, leave out the sugar and add 3–4 rashers of bacon, crisply cooked and crumbled.

Dates, chopped nuts, blueberries, orange and lemon peel are also popular additions. For a very light texture use buttermilk instead of milk.

Butter

Good butter is one of the luxuries of living in a cool climate, for good butter only comes with good pastures. The technique of butter making is straightforward: the cream is skimmed from the milk and agitated until the cream solids cohere to form butter. The liquid left in the churn is buttermilk, pleasant and cool to drink and useful in baking. The methods of agitating the cream were many and varied. Butter-making in the dairy must have been hard work, but it seems a pity that the whole process has now been so completely removed to the factory. Originally butter for immediate consumption was not salted, while that to be stored for the winter was quite heavily salted. Now we have the choice of salted or unsalted butter all the year.

GREEN BUTTER

Bread and butter with herbs was the countryman's breakfast in Tudor times. Anyone wishing to continue this pleasant tradition can try making green herb butter to spread on bread or toast.

Blanch in boiling water then chop the leaves of the following herbs: mint, watercress, spinach, parsley, marjoram, thyme. Add some chopped spring onions or chives and salt. For every two teaspoons of herbs, take 30 g (1 oz) of butter and pound well together.

FAIRY BUTTER

A recipe from Mrs Beeton.

Pound the yolks of two hard-boiled eggs with one teaspoon of orange flower water and two tablespoons of castor sugar. Combine with 120 g (4 oz) of fresh butter.

(For savoury butters and butters made with smoked fish see Chapters 6 and 8.)

29

Oatcakes, Scones, Biscuits

and Breakfast Cake

"They carry with them a broad plate of metal and behind the saddle they will have a sack full of oatmeal. They lay the plate on the fire . . . and when it is hot enough they cast the thick paste thereon and make a little cake and that they eat to the comfort of their stomachs . . . wherefore it is no marvel that they make longer journeys than other people do."

Froissart on Welsh and Scottish soldiers in the Hundred Years War

"Rose and partook of an excellent breakfast . . . there was no loaf bread but very good scones, or cakes baked with flour and butter."

Boswell, *Tour of the Hebrides with Dr Johnson*, 1773

Oatcakes

Oatcakes were a Celtic invention. They served as an alternative to bread in regions where oats grew more readily than wheat. Oatcakes are an excellent breakfast food, being quick to eat, digestible and sustaining. They can be made either on a griddle, which is traditional, or baked in the oven. A griddle is a thick iron plate, used for cooking over an open fire, but it may also be used over an electric or gas ring. The griddle should be greased for cooking batter and floured for cooking dough. Put it over a low heat while making the dough or batter so that it heats through thoroughly. To test whether it is hot enough, scatter on a little flour, which should slowly turn brown. A thick cast-iron frying pan may be substituted for a griddle.

Theodora FitzGibbon gives this traditional recipe for Welsh oatcakes in her book *A Taste of Wales*.

240 g (8 oz) fine oatmeal
2 teaspoons lard
2 teaspoons butter or margarine
½ tablespoon sugar
Pinch of salt
200 ml (⅓ pint) hot water
1 egg beaten with 1 tablespoon milk and 1 tablespoon sugar for glazing

Melt the lard and butter in the hot water and add the sugar and salt. Add the oatmeal and knead into a soft dough. Roll the ball of dough in oatmeal and break off small lumps from the main piece. Roll them in the palms of the hands and flatten to a thickness of ⅛ inch. Lightly glaze the oatcakes with the egg, milk and sugar mixture and bake them on a griddle for 7 minutes. Toast the uncooked side under the grill until just brown. Store in an airtight tin, where they will keep for months.

OATCAKES BAKED IN THE OVEN

This is not a traditional recipe but it works well. It is possible to vary the texture by using part oatflakes and part oatmeal.

300 g (10 oz) oatmeal (fine or medium)
90 g (3 oz) wholewheat flour
150 g (5 oz) butter or margarine
30–60 g (1–2 oz) sugar
1 teaspoon salt
1 heaped teaspoon baking powder
Warm water to mix

Mix the dry ingredients and rub in the butter. Add enough water to make a stiff dough and roll out on a floured board to a thickness of about half an inch. Cut into circles and transfer to a greased baking tray. Bake at 375° F (190° C, Gas mark 5) for about 20 minutes or until the oatcakes are just brown underneath.

FRIED OATCAKES

These oatcakes go well with bacon.

240 g (8 oz) coarse oatmeal
1 teaspoon salt
1 level teaspoon baking powder
Milk to mix

Mix the dry ingredients and add enough milk to make a thick dropping consistency. Fry the batter a spoonful at a time in hot oil.

Scones

Though popularly associated with teatime, scones, like soda bread, are nourishing and quick to prepare for breakfast.

PLAIN SCONES

240 g (8 oz) plain, 85% or wholewheat flour
120 g (4 oz) butter or margarine

60 g (2oz) sugar
½ teaspoon salt
1 small teaspoon bicarbonate of soda
Milk to mix

Mix the dry ingredients and rub in the butter. Add enough milk to make a soft dough which is still firm enough to roll out. Roll out the dough on a floured board, cut into circles and bake on a greased tray for about 20 minutes at 400° F (200° C, Gas mark 6). This should make about a dozen scones.

YOGHURT SCONES

½ kg (1 lb) wholewheat or 85% flour
150 g (5 oz) margarine or butter
60 g (2 oz) sugar (optional)
300 ml (½ pint) yoghurt
1 teaspoon bicarbonate of soda
1 teaspoon salt

Mix the dry ingredients and rub in the butter or margarine. Add the yoghurt and a little milk if the dough is still too dry. Roll out to a thickness of about ½ inch. Cut into rounds and place on a greased baking tray. Bake for about 20 minutes at 400° F (200° C, Gas mark 6) or until the undersides of the scones are just brown. Makes about twenty scones.

CHEESE AND BACON SCONES

240 g (8 oz) plain, or 85% flour
120 g (4 oz) strong cheddar cheese, grated
5 rashers grilled chopped bacon
120 g (4 oz) margarine or butter
1 teaspoon salt
1 teaspoon baking powder
2 teaspoons dried mustard
Milk or buttermilk to mix

Mix all the dry ingredients and rub in the butter and grated cheese. Chop the cooked bacon small and add to the mixture. Add enough milk or buttermilk to make a soft dough. Roll out, cut into circles, place on a greased baking tray and bake for about 20 minutes at 375° F (190° C, Gas mark 5).

DROP SCONES

180 g (6 oz) plain or 85% flour
30–60 g (1–2 oz) sugar
1 egg
½ teaspoon salt
1 teaspoon spice (optional)
Milk to mix

Mix the dry ingredients and add the beaten egg and enough milk to make a stiff batter of dropping consistency. To form the scones, first take a spoonful of batter and drop it on to a pile of flour. Then with floured hands, pass the scone from hand to hand and drop it on to an oiled and heated griddle. Cook for a couple of minutes on each side.

BANNOCKS

90 g (3 oz) fine oatmeal or barley meal
60 g (2 oz) wholewheat flour
1 egg
30 g (1 oz) sugar (optional)
A pinch of salt
Milk to mix

Soak the oatmeal overnight in some cold water. In the morning, mix in the other ingredients to make a creamy batter of dropping consistency. Cook the bannocks by the method described in the previous recipe.

FADGE

An old Irish recipe which has the virtue of simplicity.

240 g (8 oz) wholewheat flour
60 g (2 oz) butter
150 ml (¼ pint) milk

Melt the butter in the milk. Put the flour in a basin and make a hole in the centre. Pour in the milk and butter mixture and combine to form a stiff dough. Roll out on a well-floured board. Heat and lightly oil a griddle or thick pan. Cut the dough into small circles and cook for 2 or 3 minutes on each side.

CORN PUFFS OR POPOVERS

These scones/cakes are often eaten for breakfast in America.

120 g (4 oz) plain or wholewheat flour
120 g (4 oz) cornmeal
1 teaspoon baking powder
1 teaspoon salt
2 eggs
30 g (1 oz) melted butter
60 g (2oz) sugar (or 1 teaspoon if these are to be eaten with
  savoury food)
Milk to mix

Beat the two eggs and mix in the melted butter. Mix the dry
ingredients together and add them to the eggs and butter. Add
enough milk to make a fairly liquid batter. Beat for a few minutes
until very smooth. Grease some individual cake tins (or use paper
cake cases) and half fill them with the mixture. Set the oven at 375° F
(190° C, Gas mark 5) and put in the corn puffs while it is still cold.
Allow to cook for 30 minutes.

Biscuits

"*Bis cuit*" means in French twice cooked and biscuits were originally
made to be kept for long periods, particularly on board ship. The
twice-cooking eliminated most of the moisture which could have
turned the biscuits mouldy.

Biscuits are very quick and easy to make. If they are home-made of
good ingredients, they are nourishing enough to keep you going
through the morning. Biscuits should be stored in an airtight tin
when cooked, or an uncooked roll of dough may be kept in the fridge
and the biscuits sliced off and baked as required.

BREAKFAST BISCUITS

180 g (6 oz) plain or wholewheat flour
60 g (2 oz) ground rice
20 g (4 oz) butter
1 egg yolk
90 g (3 oz) sugar
1 teaspoon mixed spice
2 tablespoons vegetable oil

37

Soften the butter. Combine the dry ingredients and mix in the oil and butter to form a stiff dough. If it is too dry, add a little more oil. Roll out on a floured board and cut the dough into biscuit shapes. Place on a greased baking tray and bake for about 25 minutes at 375° F (190° C, Gas mark 5) or until the undersides are lightly browned.

SCOTTISH SUNDAY BISCUITS

240 g (8 oz) flour, plain or wholewheat
150 g (5 oz) butter
120 g (4 oz) sugar
30 g (1 oz) ground and 30 g (1 oz) chopped almonds
30 g (1 oz) caraway seeds (optional)
Peel of an orange and a lemon
Juice of one lemon
A little vegetable oil
½ teaspoon salt

Mix the dry ingredients together. Melt the butter slowly in a saucepan, then combine with the dry ingredients. Add the juice of the lemon and a little oil to make a dough which can be easily rolled out. Cut the biscuits into the required shapes and top with caraway seeds if liked. Bake as in the previous recipe.

OATFLAKE BISCUITS

240 g (8 oz) oatflakes
150 g (5 oz) butter
2 teaspoons honey
90 g (3 oz) finely chopped dates
½ teaspoon salt
Juice and peel of one lemon

Melt the butter in a saucepan and add the other ingredients. Mix well together. Grease a shallow tin and spread the mixture out evenly in the tin. Mark out divisions with a knife so that the biscuits will break into regular shapes when they are cooked. Bake at 325° F (170° C, Gas mark 3) for 30 minutes, but if the dates show signs of burning, cover with tin foil halfway through the cooking period.

Breakfast Cakes

This was regarded as a Sunday breakfast treat in the nineteenth century. Here is a recipe of 1861 from the *Wife's Own Book of Cookery* by Fred Bishop:

"Breakfast Cake: take ½ peck of flour rub in 1½ lb of butter, add 3 lb of currants, ½ lb sugar, ¼ oz of nutmeg, mace, cinnamon, a little salt, 1½ pints warmed cream or milk, ¼ pint of brandy, 1 pint of good ale yeast, 5 eggs. Mix well together. Bake in a moderate oven. This cake will keep a good three months."

— and another recipe of more modest proportions from the *Complete Housewife*, published in 1727:

"Take 2 lb of flour, rub into it some ½ lb of butter; then put into it some spice, a little salt, ¾ lb sugar, ½ lb raisins, stoned, ½ lb currants: make these into a cake with ½ pint of ale yeast, 4 eggs and as much warm milk as you feel convenient: mix it well together: an hour and a half will bake it. This cake is good to eat with butter."

Here is my own breakfast cake recipe, somewhat less rich:

720 g (1½ lb) wholewheat or 85% flour
180 g (6 oz) butter or margarine
15 g (½ oz) dried yeast (or 30 g/1 oz fresh)
90 g (3 oz) sugar
1 teaspoon salt
120 g (4 oz) raisins
2 level teaspoons mixed spice
Peel of one lemon
1 egg
300 ml (½ pint) milk

Mix the flour, salt and spice together. Cream the yeast with a little warm water and sugar. Rub 120 g (4 oz) of the butter into the flour. When the yeast is ready, mix it in with the flour and add the raisins, sugar and lemon peel. Warm the milk and melt the remaining 60 g (2 oz) of butter in it. Pour into the dough along with the beaten egg. Mix and knead the dough well (it should be slightly more moist than a plain bread dough, but still cohere well together). Turn into a 1 kg (2 lb) bread tin and leave to rise for about 2 hours in a warm place. When it is up to the top of the tin, bake in a hot oven 400° F (200° C, Gas mark 6) for 40 minutes. Cover with foil if the loaf shows signs of burning.

39

SALLY LUNN

A "rich French breakfast cake" as Eliza Acton describes it. Sally Lunn may be the name of the cake's eighteenth-century originator, or the name may derive from the French *"sol et lune"* — sun and moon cake.

240 g (½ lb) plain flour
½ teaspoon salt
8 g (¼ oz) dried yeast (or 15g/½ oz fresh)
120 g (4 oz) double cream
1 egg
60 g (2 oz) sugar
Peel of one lemon
½ teaspoon mixed spice

Sift the dry ingredients. Cream the yeast in a minimum of warm water with a little of the sugar. Beat the egg and cream together. Add them, along with the creamed yeast, to the flour mixture. Mix and knead well into a fairly stiff dough. Turn into a tin (a brioche mould does well) and leave to rise for 1½–2 hours. Bake in a hot oven 425° F (220° C, Gas mark 7) for about 20 minutes. While the loaf is still hot, heat 1 tablespoon of sugar with 1 tablespoon of milk and brush over the loaf. This will give a very decorative glaze.

This dough may be left to rise in a polythene-covered bowl overnight, then knocked down and transferred to a tin in the morning. After half an hour it should have risen again to the top of the tin and may then be baked and eaten hot for breakfast.

APPLE CAKE

120 g (4 oz) wholewheat flour
120 g (4 oz) plain white flour
150 g (5 oz) butter or margarine
120 g (4 oz) brown sugar
2 eggs
1 teaspoon baking powder
A pinch of salt
1 large cooking apple
Juice of a lemon
**½ teaspoon each cinnamon and ginger, mixed with 1 tablespoon
  brown sugar**

Cut the cooking apple into slices and cover with lemon juice, cinnamon, ginger and one tablespoon of sugar. Leave this aside for topping the cake. Cream the butter with the sugar and beat in the yolks of egg. In a separate bowl, mix the flours together with the baking powder and salt. Fold first the flour then the stiffly beaten egg whites into the butter mixture. Turn into a greased 1 kg (1 lb) tin and arrange the flavoured apple slices in rows along the top of the cake. Preheat the oven to 350° F (180° C, Gas mark 4) and bake for one hour. Cover the top of the cake with foil if the apples begin to burn. After taking the cake out of the oven, allow to cool in the tin before attempting to turn out.

Some American Breakfast Cakes

COTTAGE CHEESE CAKE

This cake has a pleasant and unusual texture.

180 g (6 oz) wholewheat flour
60 g (2 oz) wheatgerm
120 g (4 oz) butter or margarine
150 g (5 oz) cottage cheese
150 g (5 oz) brown sugar
2 eggs
½ teaspoon salt
1 teaspoon bicarbonate of soda
Rind of an orange and of a lemon

Soften the butter and beat it up with the cottage cheese and the sugar. Add the two beaten eggs. Sift the flour with the wheatgerm, salt and bicarbonate of soda and the finely grated rinds. Fold the flour etc. into the butter mixture. Turn into a 500 g (1 lb) bread tin and bake for 50 minutes at 350° F (180° C, Gas mark 4). Test with a skewer to make sure it is done. Turn out on to a wire rack.

CARROT CAKE

120 g (4 oz) wholewheat flour
60 g (2 oz) plain flour
120 g (4 oz) butter
2 eggs
120 g (4 oz) carrots
90 g (3 oz) sugar
1 teaspoon salt
1 teaspoon baking powder
1 teaspoon cinnamon

Beat the butter and the sugar together. Add the beaten egg. Grate the carrots and mix them in. Sift the flour, baking powder, salt and cinnamon together and fold them in to make a fairly dry mixture (the water contained in the carrots will be released during cooking). Grease a 500 g (1 lb) bread tin and turn the mixture into it. Bake in a medium oven 350° F (180° C, Gas mark 4) for 50 minutes. Cover the top of the tin with foil if the cake shows signs of burning on top. Allow to cool before turning out.

CINNAMON AND SOUR CREAM CAKE

240 g (8 oz) 85% flour
120 g (4 oz) butter or margarine
150 g (5 oz) sugar
120 g (4 oz) sour cream
90 g (3 oz) finely chopped walnuts
2 level teaspoons ground cinnamon
1 teaspoon baking powder
2 eggs
A small stick of vanilla
A pinch of salt

Leave the vanilla stick in the sugar for some hours, then remove it. Cream the butter or margarine with the sugar. Beat in the eggs and the sour cream. Mix the flour with the baking powder, salt and walnuts and fold them into the creamed butter mixture. Turn into a greased cake tin and bake in a moderate oven, 350° F (180° C, Gas mark 4), for 45 minutes. Test with a skewer to make sure the cake is cooked through.

AMERICAN BANANA BREAD

This is more of a cake than a bread.

2 large very ripe bananas
240 g (8 oz) wholewheat flour
1 teaspoon baking powder
1 teaspoon mixed spice
120 g (4 oz) butter
90 g (3 oz) brown sugar
1 egg

Cream the softened butter with the sugar and beat in the egg. Mash the bananas very well and mix them into the creamed mixture. Sift the flour with the baking powder and spice and fold it in with the other ingredients. Turn the mixture into a 500 g (1 lb) bread tin and bake at 375° F (190° C, Gas mark 5) for 40 minutes.

Cereals

"*Oats* — a grain which is generally given to horses, but in Scotland supports the people."

Dr Johnson, *Dictionary*

"Very true and where else will you find such horses and such men."

Lord Elibank

Cereals

Cereals are one of the oldest foods. Early man must have gathered cereal grains and eaten them, raw or cooked, long before he found out how to grind them and turn them into bread. Grain goes much further when it is boiled in water than when it is made into bread, thus "pottage", a dish basically made of boiled grain with the addition of some vegetables, herbs and perhaps meat, was for centuries the poor man's staple diet in England, not only for breakfast, but for the other meals in the day as well. In many parts of Africa today a similar staple diet is to be found.

Some cereals, (like oats and buckwheat) do not make good bread. Thus in Scotland and Russia where oats and buckwheat were grown as staple crops, oat porridge and kasha (buckwheat porridge) were the main sustenance of the people.

Some dietary reformers believe that it is more beneficial to eat cereal grains uncooked. Thus Dr Bircher invented his famous muesli, which has gained renewed popularity in recent years. Dr Kellogg invented "cornflakes" to improve the diet of his patients in the Battle Creek Sanatorium. His brother saw the commercial potential in his discovery and cornfalakes have been with us ever since — along with thousands of imitations and variations. Since these commerical flakes are some of the most processed of foods, it is probably a better idea to buy unadulterated cereal flakes and mix up your own cereal at home, as recommended by Dr Bircher.

PORRIDGE

The real Scottish method:

The proportion of oatmeal to water is about one cup to three. For every person, use 30 g (1 oz) of coarsely ground oatmeal and a quarter of a teaspoon of salt. Bring the water to the boil and when it is boiling steadily scatter the oatmeal into it, allowing each grain to fall separately. Stir all the time while the oatmeal is being added: ancient tradition says always stir in a clockwise direction. When the porridge begins to thicken, turn down the heat, put a lid on the pot and allow to simmer for about 20 minutes. Add the salt towards the end of the cooking time. When it is ready the porridge should be poured into hot bowls, and beside each one, a smaller bowl of cold milk should be placed. Each spoonful of hot porridge may be cooled by dipping it into the bowl of milk. The test of good porridge is for the grains of oatmeal to remain separate in the cooking.

QUICK PORRIDGE

This definitely lacks the texture of the above recipe but is still nourishing and very quick to make. Warm 300 ml (½ pint) of milk in a saucepan. Stir in three ounces of soft rolled oats. Bring up to the boil, stirring. Allow to simmer for 3 or 4 minutes over a low heat.

The chief inducement to eating porridge when I was a child was being able to draw patterns with the thin, viscous stream of golden syrup as it dropped from the spoon. Another porridge flavouring which children might enjoy is carob powder. Add one and a half teaspoonfuls to the above recipe for quick porridge.

BROSE

Another Scottish breakfast dish, well suited to the Northern winter. Melt some suet or butter in a pan and add as much oatmeal as can be absorbed. Pour over three times the volume of boiling water, stir and allow to simmer until the oats are soft.

FLUMMERY

An old English recipe quoted by Dorothy Hartley in *Food in England*:

"To make a pretty sort of Flummery: put three handfuls of fine oatmeal into two quarts of water, let it steep a day and a night, then pour off the clear water through a fine sieve and boil it down till it is as thick as hasty pudding. Put in sugar to taste and a spoonful of orange flower-water. Pour it into a shallow dish to set for your use."

Dorothy Hartley says that it makes a pleasant summer dish, in place of porridge, especially when eaten with soft fruit and cream.

OATS IN YOGHURT

My favourite way of preparing oats for breakfast — it could hardly be quicker — is to toast some "pinwheel", or coarse oats in a dry pan, then tip them, with a nice sizzling noise, into a bowl of cold yogurt. Some honey or brown sugar can be added.

AN OAT-BASED BABY CEREAL

My daughter was reared on this cereal and seemed to do very well on it. The mixture has a high Vitamin B and iron content and, in my opinion, is much better than anything that comes out of a packet.

180 g (6 oz) fine oatmeal or soft oatflakes
60 g (2 oz) wheatgerm
60 g (2 oz) sesame seeds
30 g (1 oz) soya flour

Grind the sesame seeds finely and also the oats, if flakes are being used. Mix the four ingredients very well together. This can be mixed with milk, fruit juice or puréed vegetables.

BUCKWHEAT PORRIDGE (KASHA)

This makes a very sustaining winter breakfast. Buckwheat is filling and has a reputation for keeping out the cold.

Roast one cup of buckwheat (it may also be bought ready roasted) in a dry pan. Cover with two cups of boiling water and add one teaspoon of salt. Cover the pan and leave it to simmer for about fifteen minutes. By this time the water should have been absorbed and the grain should be soft. Serve the kasha with butter — the Russians have a saying that you can't spoil good kasha with butter. It may also be eaten with mushrooms or bacon.

MILLET PORRIDGE

Millet makes a good porridge because the grain is so small.
Wash the millet well and pick out any black grains. Bring to the boil
in plenty of water and skim the surface to remove the scum. Drain
and return to the heat. To every cup of grain, add double the amount
of milk and water mixed. Cover and simmer for about 15 minutes, or
until all the water is absorbed. If it becomes too dry, add some more
milk. When cooked, add some butter and salt or sugar to taste.

SOUTHERN GRITS

This is a porridge made from coarsely-ground dried maize. It is
native to the Southern States of America.
   Bring one cup of grits to the boil in four cups of salted water. Leave
to simmer for one hour. When it is ready, the porridge may be served
with butter.

RUSSIAN BREAKFAST SEMOLINA:

120 g (4 oz) semolina
900 ml (1½ pints) milk
120 g (4 oz) sugar
½ teaspoon of salt
1 tablespoon of butter

Bring the milk and salt to the boil. Take off the heat and gradually
add the semolina, stirring all the time. Return to the heat and simmer
for five minutes, stirring. Add the sugar and butter and serve hot.

SEMOLINA WITH LEMON AND ALMONDS

This is served for breakfast in some parts of Syria:

60 g (2 oz) semolina
90 g (3 oz) sugar
30 g (1 oz) ground almonds
Juice and peel of 3 lemons
450 ml (¾ pint) water

Boil the water with the sugar and the juice and grated peel of the lemons and the ground almonds for a few minutes. Fry the semolina in the butter for a few minutes, stirring all the time. Gradually add the lemon liquid to the semolina mixture, stirring continuously. When the mixture is thoroughly combined, pour it into individual bowls and chill.

FRUMENTY

This is another old English dish which used to be made on festive occasions. Here is one of the many versions:

480 g (1 lb) wheat berries
600 ml (1 pint) milk
150 g (5 oz) ground almonds
180 g (6 oz) chopped dates, apricots and raisins, mixed
Peel of two lemons
1 teaspoon cinnamon
½ teaspoon nutmeg
Sugar or honey to taste

Put the wheat berries in a basin and cover with boiling water. Leave to stand in a warm place overnight, or longer if the wheat is still not soft. (It should be pleasantly crunchy but not too hard.) Drain the wheat and put it in a pan with the milk and all the other ingredients, except the fruit. Bring to the boil and simmer for half an hour. Add the finely-chopped dates, apricots and raisins. Eat while still hot, with cream and sugar or honey to taste.

MUESLI

Dr Bircher's recipe is simple: soak some oatflakes (the harder variety) in water overnight. In the morning add some lemon juice, grated apples, flaked almonds, honey and cream or yogurt. Other seasonal fruit can also be added.

When mixing up muesli at home, different combinations of cereal flakes, dried fruit, nuts and seeds can be used. Here are some suggestions:

51

Oats, wheat, barley or rye flakes, wheatgerm or bran.
Dried dates, figs, apricots, bananas, peaches, pears, raisins, sultanas or currants.
Almonds, peanuts, hazelnuts, walnuts, broken brazils or grated coconut.
Seasame seeds or sunflower seeds.

In summer, fresh soft fruits, like strawberries, raspberries, peaches and cherries can be mixed with the cereal grains and yogurt to make a quick and luxurious breakfast.

A FAVOURITE MUESLI RECIPE

This muesli can be made in any quantity based on the following proportions:

250 g (8 oz) soft oatflakes
150 g (5 oz) toasted ground almonds
120 g (4 oz) currants
90 g (3 oz) apricots
60 g (2 oz) wheatgerm
60 g (2 oz) brown sugar

Toast the almonds lightly under the grill and grind them finely in a coffee grinder or pestle. Chop the apricots, then mix all the ingredients together. Store in screw-top jars.

GRANOLA

This is a kind of toasted muesli which can be bought ready-made or it can be made at home in reasonably large quantities and stored for future use. Here is one possible recipe: this recipe can be made in any quantity in the following proportions:

6 cups rolled oats
1 cup peanuts
1 cup almonds
1 cup sunflower seeds
1 cup raisins
1 cup clear honey
½ cup sunflower-seed oil

Mix the grains, fruit and nuts together in a bowl. Warm the honey and oil in a saucepan and pour it into a bowl. Mix the contents thoroughly then spread the mixture on some shallow baking trays. Pre-heat the oven to 275° F (140° C, Gas mark 1) and bake for about half an hour, turning the mixture once or twice so that it cooks evenly. Cool and store in screw-top jars until required.

LIQUID CEREAL BREAKFASTS

Here are two ideas for "liquid cereal" breakfasts (though many other combinations can easily be invented). These mixtures can be beaten up the night before and quickly drunk in the morning, even by someone in a hurry. Much more sustaining than just tea or coffee. A blender will facilitate the mixing.

200 ml (⅓ pint) yoghurt, milk or buttermilk
1 large tablespoon ground almonds
1 teaspoon wheatgerm
1 small apple, chopped
1 teaspoon honey

200 ml (⅓ pint) yoghurt, milk or buttermilk
1 small banana, chopped
1 large tablespoon fine oatmeal, preferably toasted
1 teaspoon honey

PANCAKES

"Pancakes and fritters say the bells of St Peters."

Nursery rhyme, traditional

"Fritters are first heard of during the Crusades . . . the Saracens offered fritters to St Louis when they released him from prison."

Dumas, Grand Dictionnaire de cuisine

Pancakes

Pancakes are a useful breakfast food. Pancake batter improves when left to stand for some time, thus the batter can, with advantage, be mixed up in the evening and left to stand overnight. In the morning it can be cooked, almost as quickly as toast can be made.

Plain flour, or a mixture of plain and 85% wholewheat flour makes good pancakes. (Wholewheat flour is usually too heavy.) Other flours can be mixed with wholewheat flour, for example barley flour, oatmeal, cornmeal, semolina or ground rice. Use about two-thirds wholewheat flour to one-third of the other type of flour.

In Brittany, buckwheat flour is used to make delicious thin crêpes, traditional to the region. A mixture of wholewheat flour and buckwheat is easier to handle than buckwheat alone.

Always cook pancakes in a heavy, thick-bottomed pan which has been well warmed and oiled beforehand. The first pancake of the batch is often a flop, but don't be discouraged, they always improve as you go on.

Oatcakes are, of course, traditional food for Shrove Tuesday. In the Middle Ages, eggs and milk as well as meat, were prohibited foods during Lent, so dishes which used a lavish amount of these ingredients were cooked just before Lent began. (I sometimes wonder what happened to all the eggs and milk during Lent — were the eggs preserved and the milk stored as butter or cheese?)

A BASIC PANCAKE RECIPE

240 g (8 oz) flour
1 or 2 eggs
300–450 ml (½–¾) pint of milk and water, mixed
1 small teaspoon of salt

Sift the flour with the salt in a basin. Make a well in the centre of the flour and break in the egg(s). Mix well then gradually add the liquid, stirring all the time. The batter should be of a fairly thin consistency (it will thicken up a bit while standing). Beat the mixture well and leave to stand for at least an hour. Warm a thick pan over a low heat for about 10 minutes, then add a teaspoon/dessertspoonful of oil to the pan, depending on its size. Let this heat for a few minutes, then pour in a small ladle of batter, which should be thin enough to spread evenly over the bottom of the pan but should not be too runny. Fry for 2 or 3 minutes, then toss and cook the other side. Pancakes should not be more than about a quarter of an inch thick, so be careful not to put too much batter in the pan at once.

PANCAKE FILLINGS

Whether pancakes are eaten flat on the plate or rolled, there is endless scope for spreads and fillings. Lemon juice with brown sugar is an old favourite, hard to beat. In summer, mashed soft fruits, like peaches, strawberries or raspberries, with a little lemon and sugar are excellent, as is a combination of mashed banana and concentrated apple juice. Generally, a slightly sharp, fruity taste sets off the richness of the pancakes. A German pancake-filling consists of apple purée, cinnamon, grated lemon peel and raisins.

Savoury pancake-fillings including fish, cheese or bacon can also be delicious. Some suggestions are made later on in the chapter.

CREMPOG

In order to make pancakes extra light, they are sometimes leavened with yeast, bicarbonate of soda, buttermilk or yoghurt. This is a traditional Welsh pancake recipe:

180 g (6 oz) plain flour
90 g (3 oz) fine oatmeal
300 ml (½ pint) buttermilk
½ teaspoon of salt
150 ml (¼ pint) milk or water to mix

Mix the flour, salt and oatmeal together. Beat in the buttermilk and add enough water or milk to make a fairly liquid batter. Leave to stand overnight or for at least an hour. Fry about half a small cupful at a time in a hot, well-oiled pan. This batter is a bit stickier than the standard batter so do not try to make the pancakes too big. The pancakes should be crisp on the outside and fairly soft in the middle.

FRITTERS

Fritters consist usually of fruit, or occasionally vegetables, dipped in batter and fried. Make the batter a little thicker than for pancakes (see basic recipe) and perhaps add a little cream.

Bananas, sliced longways then cut in half, or apples cored then cut into thin, flat slices, make good fritters. Pineapple, apricots and peaches are other possibilities. Sweetcorn, taken off the cob, can be mixed in with the batter then fried in small fritters. For an unusual taste, wash some heads of freshly-picked elder flowers, dip them in batter and fry.

SHROVETIDE FRITTERS

240 g (8 oz) plain flour
2 eggs
30 g (1 oz) fresh yeast or 1 teaspoon dried yeast
½ teaspoon of salt
300–450 ml (½–¾) pint milk
2 grated apples
60 g (2 oz) currants
60 g (2 oz) sugar
Grated rind of a lemon
Grating of nutmeg

Mix the flour, salt, nutmeg, lemon rind and fruit together. Mix in the eggs, then the creamed yeast, then the rest of the warm milk. Leave to stand, preferably overnight and cook as small fritters in the morning.

STRAWBERRY FRITTERS

Jane Grigson recommends these in her *Fruit Book*.

½ kg (1 lb) strawberries
120 g (4 oz) plain flour
1 egg yolk and 2 egg whites
Peel and juice of 1 lemon
A pinch of salt
Water to mix

Sift the flour with the salt. Make a well in the centre and add the beaten egg yolk and the peel and juice of the lemon. Add enough water to make a smooth batter. Beat the egg whites until they are stiff, then fold them into the mixture. Dip the strawberries in the batter one by one and fry lightly in oil.

WAFFLES

Waffles were originally "wafers", a medieval luxury, often eaten at the end of a banquet. They were made of flour, egg yolk, spices, cream and sugar and baked between wafer irons, which were usually imprinted with a decorative design. Chaucer mentions "Wafers piping hot out of the gleed". Communion wafers, as taken in church, are descended from wafers and the Pilgrim Fathers must have taken some waffling irons with them to America, whence the popularity of waffles spread all over the continent.

The batter for waffles is much like that for pancakes and, similarly, there are many variations.

Here is a basic mixture for making waffles:

240 g (8 oz) flour (plain or mixed plain and wholewheat)
1 egg
½ teaspoon salt
30 g (1 oz) sugar (optional)
½ teaspoon bicarbonate of soda
30 g (1 oz) butter
150 ml (¼ pint) milk and 150 ml (¼ pint) water to mix

Mix the flour with the bicarbonate and the salt. Make a well in the centre of the mixture and pour in the beaten egg yolk. Add the water and the milk gradually, mixing all the time with a fork. Lastly, beat in the melted butter, then the stiffly-beaten egg white. Grease the waffling irons lightly and cook until the waffles are just brown on the outsides.

In some American recipes, half the flour is replaced with fine cornmeal. In others, buttermilk is used instead of milk and water.

Like pancakes, waffles may be eaten savoury or sweet. They are good eaten with ham or bacon; or they may be spread with thin slices of cheese and then toasted under the grill. Americans favour maple syrup, to which fresh crushed fruit may also be added. Mashed bananas mixed with a little concentrated apple juice is another sweet-toothed possibility.

BLINIS

These famous Russian pancakes are very light because of the yeast, buttermilk (or sour milk) and stiffly-beaten egg white, which they contain. It is possible to substitute bicarbonate of soda for the yeast and still achieve a good light texture.

120 g (4 oz) buckwheat flour
120 g (4 oz) plain wholewheat flour
½ teaspoon salt
15 g (½ oz) fresh or 30 g (1 oz) dried yeast
300 ml (½ pint) of buttermilk
2 eggs

Mix the flour, buckwheat flour and salt. Cream the yeast as for bread (see Chapter 1) in half a cup of warm water. Add to the flour then beat in the buttermilk as well. Leave, covered, to stand in a warm place for at least an hour. Beat the egg yolks into the mixture, then, having beaten the egg whites stiff, fold them in last. Warm the pan over a low heat for a few minutes; when it is hot pour in a little oil. Increase the heat and fry the pancakes lightly on either side. About two or three tablespoons of batter is enough for each pancake.

Blinis are the traditional accompaniment to caviar, but if you can't afford caviar for breakfast, they are very good with grilled bacon or any smoked fish. Finnan haddock poached in a little milk and butter and served with blinis is recommended.

PAPANAS

These pancakes are of Eastern European origin. They are very good served with a fresh fruit salad to offset their richness.

120 g (4 oz) plain flour
½ teaspoon salt
120 g (4 oz) curd cheese
120 g (4 oz) yoghurt
Yolk of 1 egg and whites of 2 eggs
Water to mix

Sift the flour and salt, make a well in the centre and drop in egg yolk. Beat the curd cheese and the yoghurt separately then add them to the flour and egg along with about half a cup of water. Beat well together. Whip the egg whites and fold them into the mixture. The batter should be of a stiff dropping consistency. Heat a pan containing a little oil and fry the batter, about a tablespoon at a time, as small, flat cakes.

GERMAN BACON PANCAKES

These were apparently cooked at harvest time in Germany to give extra energy to the harvesters.

240 g (8oz) plain flour
2 eggs
15 g (½ oz) fresh yeast (or 1 teaspoon dried)
300–450 ml (½–¾ pint) milk and water mixed
½ teaspoon salt

Sift the flour with the salt and mix in the beaten eggs. Dissolve the yeast in a little of the warmed water and add to the batter. Gradually add the rest of the warmed liquid and leave the mixture to stand in a warm place for at least an hour. Fry two rashers of bacon on one side over a low heat, turn them over and pour on a small cupful of the pancake batter. Fry for 2 or 3 minutes, toss and finish cooking on the other side.

PANCAKES CALLED "A QUIRE OF PAPER"

This is an eighteenth-century recipe given by Hannah Glasse:

"Take a pint of cream, six eggs, three spoonfuls of fine flour, three of sack, one of orange-flower water, a little sugar, and half a nutmeg grated, half a pound of melted butter almost cold. Mingle all well together and butter the pan for the first pancake, then let them run as thin as possible; when they are just coloured they are enough."

INSTANT ORANGE JUICE PANCAKES

300 ml (½ pint) orange juice
180 g (6 oz) brown flour
1 egg
1 tablespoon oil

Beat the egg in a bowl and add the orange juice, oil and flour. Mix the ingredients well together. Heat up a pan with a little oil and fry the batter, two or three tablespoons at a time. The batter should be fairly liquid and the pancakes as thin and light as possible.

DOSAIS

These pancakes made from the flour of rice and lentils are a very popular breakfast in Southern India. White lentils are generally used, but I have used ground brown lentils quite successfully. The proportion of rice flour to pulse flour may be varied. Dosais are often stuffed with a spicy potato mixture, similar to that used for filling parathas (see page), or they may be eaten with any Indian chutney or sambhar (a tasty mixture of split peas, spices and vegetables).

150 g (5 oz) rice flour
150 g (5 oz) ground lentils (urid dhal or other lentil flour)
2 teaspoons salt
300 ml (½ pint) water or buttermilk

If grinding the flours at home, soak the rice and lentils in separate bowls all day. Then drain and grind the rice in a coffee grinder and the lentils in a liquidizer with a little water. Put both flours into a bowl and cover with 300 ml (½ pint) water or buttermilk. Leave to stand overnight. In the morning beat the mixture and add more liquid if necessary to obtain a thick dropping consistency. Heat a skillet or thick pan, oil it lightly and fry the pancakes as thinly as possible.

EGGS

"Staid at the King's Head (Southwark) and eat a breakfast of eggs."

Pepys, *The Diary of Samuel Pepys* 1882

Eggs

Eggs were regarded by the ancient Greeks as a symbol of the Universe, a sacred symbol of life. Followers of Pythagoras refused to eat eggs on this account. The Druids dyed eggs different colours and used them in their springtime ceremonies celebrating the New Year. The Christians took over this custom and Easter eggs became the symbol of the Resurrection.

The eating of eggs for breakfast seems to have become popular in the eighteenth century, but the Victorians really made it into a ritual. Individual saucepans with spirit-burners were made for the breakfast table so that each person could boil his egg to his satisfaction; or else a number of eggs were brought to the table in large chicken dishes containing hot water to keep the eggs warm. Egg timers, cosies, egg spoons and egg cups completed the paraphernalia.

Boiled Eggs

Mrs Beeton says that "eggs for boiling cannot be too fresh or boiled too soon after they are laid". With great scientific accuracy, she reveals the secret of boiling an egg without cracking it: "When fresh eggs are dropped into a vessel full of boiling water, they crack because the eggs, being well filled, the shells give way to the interior fluids dilated by the heat. If the volume of water be small, the shells do not crack because the temperature is lowered by the eggs before the interior dilation can take place."

To allay controversy over how long eggs should be boiled to produce the various degrees of hardness and softness, here is a table given by the British Egg Information Service:

	Large egg	Small egg
Soft-boiled	3 mins	2¼ mins
Hard white and soft yolk	4½ mins	3 mins
Hard-boiled	8 mins	6 mins

Those who like soft eggs but have bad memories can "coddle" their eggs: boil the water in a pan, remove it from the heat and put in the eggs. Put a lid on the pan and leave it for six to eight minutes depending on the size of the egg.

HAMINE EGGS

This is an ancient recipe described by Claudia Roden in *Middle Eastern Cookery*; it is still, she says, often prepared as a picnic food in the Middle East:

"Put the eggs with the skins from several onions together in a very large saucepan. Fill the pan with water, cover and simmer very gently on the lowest possible heat for at least six hours, even overnight. A layer of oil poured over the surface is a good way of preventing the water from evaporating too quickly. This lengthy cooking produces delicious creamy eggs. The whites acquire a soft beige colour from the onion skins and the yolks are a very creamy pale yellow."

FRICASSEE OF EGGS

Hard-boil four eggs, peel them and chop them up. Clean and chop 120 g (¼ lb) of mushrooms and turn them in a hot oil and butter mixture with a little garlic if liked. Add the chopped eggs, seasoned with salt and pepper and 1–2 tablespoons of fresh chopped herbs if possible. Add 3–4 tablespoons single cream, stir well and cook for a couple of minutes longer.

ROASTED EGGS

The precursors of boiled eggs were roasted eggs. In the days of wood fires when it would have taken a lot of time and fuel to boil a pan of water, eggs were simply put into the embers of the fire to cook in their shells. I found that roasted eggs were rather tough and not really an improvement on boiled ones. However, they are worth a try if you are baking something else in the oven at the same time: prick the eggs at the round end with a needle and place them on a wire rack in the oven. At a temperature of about 300° F (150° C, Gas mark 2) hard roasted eggs will take about 15 minutes and soft about 12 minutes. No doubt eggs roasted on a camp fire would be absolutely delicious, since food cooked outdoors always tastes better anyway. When you have eaten your boiled or roasted egg, don't forget to crush the shell in case a witch should use it as a boat!

Poached Eggs

To poach eggs without having them disintegrate first, dip the eggs in boiling water for a few seconds before cracking them. Have ready a saucepan with about three inches of water brought to the boil. Lower the heat so that the water is simmering and break the eggs into it gently. Allow to cook for three or four minutes.

CREAM SAUCE FOR POACHED EGGS

Allow one tablespoon of cream for each egg, season with salt and pepper and mustard and any fresh chopped herbs which are available. Bring to the boil and add 1 teaspoon of butter for every tablespoon of cream.

POACHED EGGS IN YOGHURT

Season some yoghurt with paprika and salt and a little fresh chopped mint. Pour it into small bowls. Poach the required number of eggs and drop each one into a bowl of yogurt. Pour a little melted butter over each egg.

OEUFS EN COCOTTE

Break the eggs into individual china dishes. Season with salt and pepper. Place the dishes in a shallow pan of boiling water so that the water comes about halfway up to the top of the dishes and continue to boil the water until the eggs are set.

EGGS BENEDICT

Take one large English muffin (recipe on page 27). Toast it on both sides and break it open into equal halves. Put a thick slice of ham and a poached egg on each half.

Fried Eggs

Eggs should be fried in a little oil or fat, not so quickly that the bottom burns before the top is solid. If you fry them rather slowly with a lid over the pan, the yolks and whites will cook to a nice consistency. Sprinkle salt and pepper and grated cheese over the eggs at the beginning of cooking for extra taste.

FRIED CHEESE AND EGGS

Cut slices of Edam or Gouda cheese about a quarter of an inch thick. Dip them in flour and fry them in oil for about 2 minutes. Turn the slices over and break an egg on each slice. Continue to cook until the whites are solid.

PAIN PERDU

A good way to make one egg go between two people.

In a basin, beat up an egg with some seasoning and dip into it a slice of bread which has been pricked all over with a fork. Leave it for a few minutes to soak up half of the egg mixture and then fry in a little oil and butter on both sides. Repeat the process with the second slice of bread.

Scrambled Eggs

For a plain scrambled egg, use a dessertspoon each of milk and butter to each egg. Melt the butter slowly in a thick pan and beat the eggs in a basin with the milk and any desired seasoning. When the butter is melted, pour the egg mixture into the pan and stir continuously. Take the pan off the heat just before the eggs are set, because they will go on cooking in the heat of the pan.

As a variation, the eggs may be mixed with a little cream or sour cream instead of milk.

LA PIPARRADA

A Spanish version of scrambled eggs from the Basque country:

1 onion
3 green peppers
360 g (¾ lb) tomatoes
4 eggs
1–2 cloves of garlic (optional)
Salt and pepper and fresh basil if available

Finely chop the garlic and onion and fry in some oil or butter, over a low heat. Remove the seeds from the peppers and chop into fine strips, add them to the pan and fry for about five minutes. Meanwhile, dip the tomatoes in boiling water and remove the skins. Chop them roughly and put them into the pan. Let them cook until they are quite pulpy, then pour in the beaten, seasoned eggs. Continue to cook until the eggs are almost solid, then remove from the heat.

Less elaborate scrambled-egg recipes may be prepared by frying chopped bacon, mushrooms or ham and stirring in the eggs when they are almost cooked.

Baked Eggs

Also known as *"œufs sur le plat"*. Each egg is broken into a small, greased oven-proof dish, topped with a little butter and baked for 8–12 minutes in a hot oven.

ŒUFS BONNE FEMME

240 g (½ lb) mushrooms
4 slices of bread cut into circles
4 eggs
90 g (3 oz) oil and butter mixed
60 g (2 oz) grated cheese
Salt and pepper

Set the oven at 350° F (180° C, Gas mark 4). Fry the bread on both sides in oil. Ideally, take four very large field mushrooms, remove the stalks and soften them in a little butter. If such large mushrooms are not available, take 250 g (½ lb) of smaller ones, chop them and soften them and cook them lightly in the same way. Put the fried bread on to a greased oven dish and arrange the mushrooms, seasoned with salt and pepper, on top of them. Carefully break an egg over each piece of bread and sprinkle generously with Parmesan or other grated cheese. Bake for 10–15 minutes or until the egg whites are set.

A "Herbolace" was a popular medieval dish. Seasonal fresh herbs were chopped or shredded and mixed with some beaten eggs. This mixture was then baked in the oven in a shallow dish.

Omelettes

Plain omelettes are made by beating up the whole egg with the desired seasoning and pouring the mixture into a hot pan containing a little oil. They should be fried until almost brown on one side, then folded in half and cooked for another couple of minutes. Mrs Beeton says that an omelette should never be turned, like a pancake, but rather, if the top is under-done, it should be browned under the grill.

Soufflé omelettes are similarily cooked, but the egg yolk is separated from the white at the outset and the latter beaten stiffly before being folded into the beaten yolk. The mixture is then immediately turned into the pan.

When making a filled omelette, cook the filling before mixing up the eggs and leave it aside in a warm place. Add it to the omelette just before folding, so that it is nicely enclosed between the two halves.

ELIZABETH DAVID'S MUSHROOM FILLING FOR OMELETTES

Cook 360 g (¾ lb) of mushrooms in butter with some salt and pepper and a little nutmeg. Stir in a pinch of flour and two tablespoons of cream. Add to the omelette just before folding in half.

MRS BEETON'S RECIPE FOR KIDNEY OMELETTE

This omelette is cooked all together. Skin and dice the kidneys. Toss them in butter for 2 or 3 minutes. Mix them in with the whisked eggs. Cook the omelette in the usual way.

SPANISH POTATO OMELETTE

4 eggs
4 medium potatoes, cooked and diced
2 tablespoons olive oil
1 tablespoon butter
1 onion
1 tablespoon chopped parsley

Heat the oil and butter in a pan and fry the chopped onion until golden. Add the potatoes and cook for a further couple of minutes. Beat up the eggs with the chopped parsley, salt and pepper. Pour over the onion and potato mixture. Cook until the eggs are just set.

OMELETTE ARNOLD BENNETT

The writer was accustomed to eat this when he had supper at the Savoy, but it is equally good eaten for breakfast (the cream can be omitted).

6 eggs
240 g (½ lb) smoked haddock (filleted)
2 tablespoons grated Parmesan cheese
3 tablespoons double cream
Salt and pepper

Poach the haddock in a little milk, drain it and flake into small pieces. Mix in the grated Parmesan. Make a soufflé omelette, seasoned with salt and pepper and cook it without folding. While the omelette is still moist on top, pile on the fish and cheese mixture and finally the cream. Put under a hot grill for a few minutes to finish cooking.

73

A SWEET OMELETTE

Thinly slice two bananas and soften them in a pan with a little butter. Add a teaspoon of brown sugar if liked. Make a soufflé omelette with the four eggs. Add the banana filling just before folding the omelette and finish by browning under a hot grill.

OMELETTE FINES HERBES

Finely chop some parsley, tarragon, chives and chervil and beat them up with the eggs and seasoning.

Chopped crispy bacon, chopped blanched sorrel and asparagus tips also make excellent fillings for a breakfast omelette.

Raw Eggs

For a very quick yet nourishing breakfast, the yolk of a raw egg may be beaten up or liquidized with various ingredients. The amounts given are for one person.

TWO EGG AND FRUIT FLIPS

150 ml (¼ pint) milk
150 ml (¼ pint) apple juice
1 egg yolk
½ banana, sliced or mashed

150 ml (¼ pint) yoghurt
1 tablespoon of honey
1 egg yolk
150 ml (¼ pint) pineapple juice

Mrs Beeton suggests beating up an egg yolk and gradually pouring over it a very hot cup of tea or coffee.

Alternatively, equal quantities of cold black coffee and yoghurt can be mixed with the yolk of an egg.

The classic recipe for those suffering from a hangover is:

1 egg yolk
1 tablespoon Worcester sauce
2 tablespoons tomato juice
½ teaspoon vinegar
A little salt and pepper

Beat the ingredients well together.

Eggs — other than Hens'

Chickens are the most prolific layers of eggs, having been thus bred for many centuries. However, geese, ducks, guinea fowl and plovers also produce eggs which humans deem worthy of consumption. Alexander Dumas, père, writing in the nineteenth century, describes how French zoos would supply the eggs of exotic birds to the gourmets of the time. Seagulls eggs were once commonly eaten in England as were the eggs of many other wild birds.

One Victorian recipe book which I consulted suggested that a basket of plovers' eggs (hard-boiled), presented in a basket lined with moss, would provide a pretty decoration for the breakfast table.

Storing Eggs

Eggs can be stored in salt or in isinglass but the simplest method is to cover the shells with cooking fat and store the eggs (in egg boxes) in a cool place. Someone told me that he used to receive eggs preserved in this way from Australia during the war.

As a town dweller, I am often amazed how delicious — and cheap — free-range eggs bought directly from the farm can be. If the hens are laying well, it is worth buying dozens of eggs from a good farm and storing them in the way described.

Hearty Breakfasts

"One goose, one turkey, one snipe, one grouse, two woodcocks, one pheasant, two partridges, one and a half bullocks' tongues, half a hare, one pound of grated ham, one pint of good gravy, seven pounds of flour, one and a quarter pounds of suet, two pounds of butter."

Contents of a "Game Pie for a Hunting Breakfast"
from a Victorian recipe book

Meat was consumed in alarming quantities at breakfast time in Victorian and Edwardian England. Mrs Beeton recommended "Mutton chops, rump steak, broiled sheep's kidneys, sausages and rashers of bacon" as suitable hot dishes, with "collared and potted meats, cold game or poultry, veal and ham pies, game and rump steak pies" as cold dishes, all "nicely garnished" on the sideboard. Devilled phesasant was also popular, and in Scotland one might have been confronted with a singed sheep's head — not the best possible way to start the day, one might think.

Cheese has always been less common in England at breakfast time but is very usual in Germany and Holland. Very thin slices of Edam or Gouda with crisp rye biscuits can be very good for breakfast. One friend assures me that the best possible breakfast consists of Welsh Rarebit and black coffee.

Ham or bacon combine very well with cheese at any time in the day and several of the following recipes use both ingredients.

Ham and Bacon

In England, York is noted for its ham and Wiltshire for its bacon. The original fine flavour of York ham was attributed to its being smoked over oak shavings left over from the building of York Minster. The preparation of ham and bacon now usually takes place in a factory, but, not so long ago, the art of curing bacon at home was widely known. First the bacon was pickled in brine and all the impurities removed. It was then "cured" in a mixture of water, saltpetre, salt and sugar. There are many different curing mixtures, which gave the distinctive regional flavours. The curing takes up to a month to be completed and the bacon is then ready to be smoked. In the old days it was enough to hang the joints from the kitchen ceiling, where they became sufficiently imbued with smoke from the open fire.

BACON AND EGGS

Cook the bacon slowly for seven to eight minutes on one side. Turn it over and break the eggs in the same pan. Add a little oil if there is insufficient bacon fat for them to cook in. Cook for a further 6 or 7 minutes. The eggs will have a nice texture if the pan is covered with a lid.

MIXED GRILL

The components of a mixed grill may vary. In Victorian times, a chop was considered essential. Now bacon, ham or sausages are more usual, plus mushrooms, tomatoes, fried potatoes or fried bread. To add an interesting savour to a mixed grill, serve it with devilled butter (see recipe on page 36)

RASTONS

6 large rolls
6 rashers of bacon, cooked and finely chopped
180 g (6 oz) mushrooms
90 g (3 oz) grated cheese
Salt and pepper

Cut off the tops of the rolls and scoop out the insides. Fry and chop the bacon. Crumble the bread and fry the crumbs in the bacon fat. Wash and chop the mushrooms small, add a little oil to the pan and sauté the mushrooms quickly for a couple of minutes. Combine the bacon, breadcrumbs and mushrooms with the grated cheese, season with pepper. Fill the hollow rolls with the mixture and place them in a hot oven for 10 minutes.

CROQUE MONSIEUR

This is a common lunch-time snack on the Continent, but it is also suitable for a hearty breakfast. Here is one version of the recipe:

A good slice of ham
2 slices of bread
2 slices of cheese (Edam or Gouda are suitable)
1 beaten egg yolk
Mustard, salt and pepper

Spread the ham with some mustard. Cut two fairly thick slices of cheese, sandwich the ham between them and sprinkle with pepper. Prick the slices of bread all over with a fork and dip them in the beaten egg yolk. When the egg has been absorbed by the bread, sandwich the cheese and ham between the slice. Melt some oil and butter in a pan and fry over a medium heat for about 5 minutes on each side. The outside should be fried just brown and the cheese should be slightly melted.

ELIZA ACTON'S CHEESE AND HAM SNACK

"Cut some slices of bread free from crust, about ½ inch thick and 2½ inches square. Butter the tops thickly, spread a little mustard on them and cover with a deep layer of grated cheese and minced ham, rather highly seasoned with cayenne. Fry them in good butter, do not turn them in the pan; place them in a Dutch oven (i.e. under the grill) for 3–4 minutes to melt the cheese. Serve them very hot."

Sausages

The advantage of making sausages at home is that you know exactly what has gone into them and you can flavour them interestingly with herbs and spices.

. A basic way of making sausages is to mince the meat (which is usually pork or beef) and mix it with an equal quantity of bread crumbs. Season with salt and pepper, herbs and spices and press the mixture into skins, which can be obtained from some butchers.

To make a more "continental" tasting sausage, add plenty of garlic, paprika or peppercorns.

EPPING SAUSAGES

1 kg (2 lb) pork
1 kg (2 lb) beef suet
2 teaspoons chopped sage leaves
1 teaspoon thyme
1 teaspoon marjoram
Rind of two lemons
½ teaspoon nutmeg
Pepper and salt
2 beaten eggs

Trim the pork of all skin and fat and mince it with the beef suet. Mix the herbs and spices very well. Press into a loaf shape and keep in the refrigerator until required. Then combine with the beaten eggs and form into sausage shapes. Fry in hot oil. There is no need to use sausage skins as the mixture has a firm consistency.

CUMBERLAND SAUSAGES

These sausages are chiefly made of pork. Here is a recipe from Mary Norwak's *The Farmhouse Kitchen* (herbs may be varied to taste).

750 g (1½ lb) lean and fat pork
180 g (6 oz) bread
Salt and pepper
A pinch of marjoram
Sausage skins (optional)

"Mince the pork twice. Soak the bread in cold water until very wet and mix this with the pork. Add the salt and pepper and marjoram. Put into skins or form into sausage shapes for frying."

Hannah Glasse quotes this eighteenth-century recipe:

"Take a pound of lean veal, one pound of young pork, fat and lean, free of skin and gristle; one pound of beef suet, half the peel of a lemon shredded very fine, half a pound of breadcrumbs, a grated nutmeg, six sage leaves, washed and chopped very fine; one teaspoon of pepper, two of salt, some thyme, savory and marjoram shred fine. Mix well together and put it close down in a pan. When you use it roll out the size of a common sausage and fry them in fresh butter of a fine brown or broil them over a clear fire and send them to the table as hot as possible."

GLAMORGAN SAUSAGES

"The breakfast was delicious, consisting of excellent tea, buttered toast and Glamorgan sausages, which are, I think, not a whit inferior to those of Epping."

George Borrow, *Wild Wales.*

120 g (4 oz) cheese (Edam or Gouda are suitable)
120 g (4 oz) brown breadcrumbs
1 small onion
2 eggs (separated)
1 teaspoon mustard powder
2 teaspoons finely chopped parsley
A few sprigs of fresh herbs, e.g. thyme, savory, oregano, if available.
A little pepper

Grate the breadcrumbs, cheese and onion and mix them together. Chop the parsley and herbs and beat the egg yolks. Combine all the ingredients and season with salt, pepper and mustard powder. Add a little water if the mixture is too dry. Shape into sausages or rissoles. Dip into the separated egg white and then into the breadcrumbs. Fry over a medium heat in a little oil and butter until the outsides are just brown.

Kidneys

"Kidneys were on his mind as he moved about the kitchen, softly righting her breakfast things on the humpy tray . . ."

James Joyce, Leopold Bloom in *Ulysses*

Theodora FitzGibbon in *A Taste of Ireland* recommends kidneys to be prepared in the following way:

"Allow 2–3 kidneys per person. Put the kidneys, still in their casing of fat, in a baking dish, cook for thirty minutes at 350° F (180° C, Gas mark 4). Break open and serve with salt and pepper on toast."

Another way of preparing kidneys is as follows:

240 g (8 oz) kidneys (lambs)
120 g (4 oz) butter
120 g (4 oz) mushrooms
2 small onions
2 teaspoons fresh herbs (thyme, sage, parsley)
Juice of a lemon
Salt and pepper

Skin the kidneys and slice them. Chop the onions, simmer them in butter for a few minutes, then add the kidneys. Continue to cook for another 5 minutes and add the herbs, lemon juice, salt and pepper. Allow to simmer for a few minutes more. Transfer the contents of the pan to a dish and keep warm while sautéing the mushrooms in the juices left in the pan. Mix the mushrooms with the kidneys and serve with hot buttered toast.

A *few* Cheese Recipes

WELSH RAREBIT

120 g (4 oz) hard English cheese
30 g (1 oz) butter
1 teaspoon liquid mustard
1 tablespoon cream (optional)

Melt the butter in a pan and stir in the grated cheese and the mustard. Stir until the cheese is melted; add a tablespoon of cream if liked. Pour the mixture on to the untoasted side of rounds of toast and grill until the cheese is just turning brown.

If a poached egg is added to the above Welsh Rarebit, it becomes Buckinghamshire Rarebit. The original English Rarebit consisted of bread soaked in red wine, then toasted, then covered with cheese and toasted again. I think they must have used a very sweet red wine, because when I tried the recipe using vin ordinaire, the result was unpleasantly bitter.

KENTISH RAREBIT

Fry two eating apples, peeled and sliced in a little butter. When they are soft, mix in 250 g (8 oz) of grated cheese and stir the mixture until the cheese is melted. Pour the mixture on to the untoasted side of rounds of toast and put them under the grill to brown.

APPLE AND CHEESE GALETTE

Another good cheese and apple combination.

240 g (8 oz) plain or wholewheat flour
½ teaspoon salt
150 g (5 oz) butter
150 g (5 oz) cheese
1 large cooking apple
30–60 g (1–2 oz) brown sugar

Mix the flour and the salt and rub in the butter, then the grated cheese. Make into a dough by adding a few drops of water. Leave to cool in the refrigerator for an hour or more (this dough can also be prepared overnight). Next roll out the dough into two large circles. Peel, core and slice the apple and put onto one of the circles. Sprinkle with sugar and cover with the other circle. Press the edges of the pastry together with finger and thumb, place on a greased baking tray and bake in a hot oven, 425° F (220° C, Gas mark 7), for 15–20 minutes. Serve hot.

CHEESE FRITTERS

120 g (4 oz) wholewheat flour
60 g (2 oz) butter
2 eggs
120 g (4 oz) grated cheese
A little mustard and pepper

Boil the butter in 150 ml (¼ pint) of water. Add the grated cheese, beaten eggs, flour and seasoning. Beat all the ingredients into a smooth batter. Heat some oil in a pan and fry the fritters spoonful by spoonful for a couple of minutes on each side. These fritters may be served with bacon and mushrooms.

Some Savoury Spreads and Relishes

DEVILLED BUTTER

90 g (3 oz) butter
½ teaspoon paprika
½ teaspoon curry powder
Salt spoon of ground black pepper
Pinch of cayenne

Combine all the ingredients well together with a fork. Serve on toast, or as an accompaniment to a mixed grill.

CHEESE AND BACON SPREAD

5 rashers bacon
150 g (5 oz) cheese
Small bunch of chives or six spring onions
120 g (4 oz) butter

Mince the bacon and grate the cheese finely. Chop the chives or spring onions very small. Mash all the ingredients together with a fork. Toast some rounds of bread on one side and spread the untoasted side with the mixture. place under a fairly low grill for 10–15 minutes, giving the bacon time to cook through. This spread may be stored in the refrigerator and used as required.

HAM BUTTER

Pound 180 g (6 oz) of minced ham together with 120 g (4 oz) butter. Season with cayenne.

CHEESE AND EGG SPREAD

120 g (4 oz) grated cheese
2 hard-boiled yolks of egg
60 g (2 oz) butter
1 teaspoon liquid mustard

Pound the ingredients together and spread on to hot buttered toast as required.

WORCESTER SAUCE

This sauce makes a piquant accompaniment to mixed grills and other savoury breakfast dishes. According to David and Rose Mabey in *Jams, Pickles and Chutneys*: "It started life in the nineteenth century as Lord Sandy's sauce . . . the story is that the recipe was given to Mr Lea of Lea and Perrins by Baron Sandys of Worcester, who picked it up when in India . . . until very recently the manufacturers kept the precise ingredients a secret; consequently there have been numerous imitations and this is one such recipe:

60 g (2 oz) shallots
4 cloves of garlic
2 teaspoons freshly grated horseradish
2 teaspoons cayenne pepper
6 cloves
4 pieces bruised root ginger
6 cardamon seeds
10 black peppercorns
30 ml (2 fluid oz) soy sauce
600 ml (1 pint) malt vinegar
2 teaspoons sugar (optional)

"Chop the shallots and garlic roughly and boil them for 15 minutes in the vinegar. Then add all the other ingredients and boil for another half-hour. Keep the lid on the sauce during boiling. Transfer to a wide-mouthed bottle, cover and leave for a month. During this time you should shake the bottle occasionally. After a month, strain the sauce through a fine sieve and re-bottle. It is now ready for use."

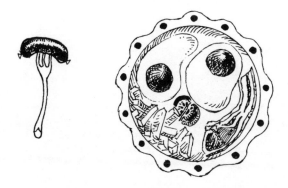

VEGETABLES

"Evening orts [left-overs] are good morning fodder."

Scottish proverb

In the Middle East tomatoes, aubergines, peppers and onions are often eaten for breakfast. In India, breakfast parathas and idlis are stuffed with vegetables. In Israel and Japan, raw salads are taken. In England however, the only vegetables commonly to appear on the breakfast table are potatoes, mushrooms and tomatoes. Potatoes can make a welcome change from the habitual cereals and pre-cooked potatoes left over from the night before, can be transformed into a variety of interesting breakfast dishes. Anyone who has gathered mushrooms early on a summer or autumn morning will appreciate the virtues of eating mushrooms for breakfast. They are never more delicious than when found wild and eaten fresh. Luckily however, for those of us not able to gather our own mushrooms very often, there are many ways of enhancing the flavour of cultivated mushrooms with good cooking. Another native speciality included in this chapter is laverbread, a prepared seaweed quite common in Wales but little known in England. It is worth seeking out since it is very tasty and highly nutritious.

Potatoes

BOXTY

This is a traditional Irish dish.

240 g (½ lb) grated raw potatoes
240 g (½ lb) cooked mashed potatoes
180 g (6 oz) wholewheat flour
1 teaspoon salt
Buttermilk to mix (or ordinary milk plus 1 teaspoon bicarbonate of soda)

Grate the raw potatoes on to a clean cloth or kitchen paper. Press out as much moisture as possible. Mix in the cooked, mashed potatoes, flour and salt and enough milk or buttermilk to form a batter of dropping consistency. Fry as small pancakes in hot fat for about 4 minutes on each side or until golden brown.

POTATO CAKES

Another Irish recipe — the Irish have many ways with potatoes.

240 g (10 oz) mashed potatoes
180 g (6 oz) self-raising flour
60 g (2 oz) butter
150 ml (¼ pint) milk
1 teaspoon salt
1 teaspoon caraway seeds
1 beaten egg

Mix all the ingredients, except the caraway seeds, together. Press into a shallow greased baking tin, top with caraway seeds and bake in a hot oven, 425° F (220° C, Gas mark 7), for twenty minutes. Split and eat hot with butter.

ANOTHER POTATO CAKE RECIPE

This recipe is good for using up all manner of left-overs.

240 g (8 oz) potatoes
60 g (2 oz) flour
60 g (2 oz) grated cheese
1 beaten egg
1 teaspoon made mustard
Milk to mix
Optional — grated carrots and onions, chopped parsley, mint, any cooked green vegetables

Combine all the ingredients and form them into small cakes about 1½ inches thick. Coat them with flour and fry on both sides until golden brown.

SCOTS POTATO FRITTERS

¾ kg (1½ lb) par-boiled potatoes
2 egg yolks
2 or 3 rashers minced bacon
Salt and pepper
60 g (2 oz) breadcrumbs

Cut the potatoes into slices. Mix the egg yolk with the minced bacon and season with salt and pepper. Dip the potato slices, first into the egg mixture, then into the breadcrumbs. Fry for a couple of minutes on each side in hot oil.

BUBBLE AND SQUEAK

The English answer to left-over potatoes. Chop and fry an onion until golden brown, then add equal quantities of mashed potatoes and cooked cabbage (other greens may also be used). Season with salt and pepper and fry over a medium heat, stirring, for about five minutes. Any left-over meat or bacon may also be chopped small and added to the mixture.

This down-to-earth recipe may be contrasted with one given by the eighteenth-century writer Hannah Glasse, where boiled mashed potatoes are mixed with "yolks of egg, a little sugar, sack, mace, nutmeg and cream; they are then made into little cakes, fried and served with more sack and sugar."

HASH BROWNS

These are an American favourite.

500 g (1 lb) par-boiled potatoes
1 medium-sized onion
2 tablespoons chopped parsley
Paprika, salt and pepper
150 ml (¼ pint) milk
1 tablespoon each butter and oil

Dice the potatoes. Heat a pan containing the oil and butter and add the onion and the potatoes. Cook over a slow heat for ten to fifteen minutes, stirring enough to prevent sticking. Mix in the parsley, milk and seasoning and cook for another 5 minutes.

CROQUETTES

Mix some cooked potatoes with butter, a little milk and seasoning. Add either grated cheese, chopped bacon, mushrooms or smoked fish, mash well together and roll the mixture into small balls with the palm of the hand. Dip the balls first into the beaten yolk of egg then into the flour or breadcrumbs. Fry in hot fat until the outsides are crisp.

NORWEGIAN FLATBRØD

Mix equal quantities of rye flour and mashed potatoes with a teaspoon of salt. Roll the mixture out on a well-floured board to a thickness of about half an inch. Cut into circles and cook in a slightly oiled pan over a medium heat. Serve with butter or sour cream.

JANSSON'S TEMPTATION

This is a simplified version of a well-known supper dish. This recipe, is less rich and quicker to make than the original, therefore more suitable for breakfast.

¾ kg (1½ lb) cooked potatoes
1 tin of anchovies
150 ml (¼ pint) milk and cream, mixed

Slice the potatoes and cover half of them with anchovies and their oil. Put the rest of the sliced potatoes in another layer on top and pour over the milk and cream mixture. Dot with butter and place under a medium grill for 10 to 15 minutes.

Mushrooms

The quickest way of cooking mushrooms is to wash, peel and slice them and then turn them in a mixture of oil and butter over a high heat. Use a thick-bottomed frying-pan and season with salt and pepper and a little garlic if liked.

Large field mushrooms are delicious baked or grilled. They should be basted with a little bacon fat or oil as they cook.

The Russians, who are still great mushroom-gatherers, sometimes cook mushrooms by dipping them in hot water for a few seconds, drying them, coating them with egg and breadcrumbs and finally frying them in hot oil.

HERB AND LEMON MUSHROOMS

240 g (½ lb) mushrooms
Juice of one lemon
1 tablespoon chopped parsley
1 teaspoon chopped thyme
Salt and pepper

Wash, peel and slice the mushrooms. Heat a thick-bottomed frying pan with a little oil and butter. Put the mushrooms with the lemon juice and herbs into the pan. Season with salt and pepper and cook over a medium heat for 5 minutes.

MUSHROOMS IN SOUR CREAM

½ kg (1 lb) mushrooms
150 ml (¼ pint) sour cream
2 tablespoons butter
1 teaspoon flour
2–3 tablespoons grated cheese
Salt and pepper

Wash, peel, chop and scald the mushrooms in boiling water for a few seconds. Drain them and place in a hot pan with the butter. Season with salt and pepper. Turn the mushrooms over a medium heat for 3 or 4 minutes, then blend in the flour and add the sour cream. Bring the mixture to the boil then place the pan under the grill. Top with grated cheese and allow the cheese to melt before serving.

95

MUSHROOM AND ANCHOVY SAVOURY

Wash, peel and chop the mushrooms and cook them rapidly in a little oil and butter. Add a few anchovies to the pan and one or two tablespoons of thick cream. Serve hot on toast.

MUSHROOM KETCHUP

This is a good thing to make when mushrooms are in glut. The resulting ketchup is strong, salty and a good flavouring to be added sparingly to many breakfast and supper dishes.

1½ kg (3 lb) mushrooms
3 tablespoons sea salt
1 teaspoon black pepper
1 teaspoon allspice
½ teaspoon nutmeg or mace
½ teaspoon ground cloves
1 pint white vinegar

Roughly chop the mushrooms and put them in a bowl. Strew them with salt and leave the bowl in a warm place for about 24 hours. Press the mushrooms with a wooden spoon from time to time to encourage the juice to flow. Next day, put the mushrooms, spices and one third of a pint of vinegar in a pan and bring the ingredients to the boil. Allow to simmer for half an hour. Add the remaining vinegar. Press the mixture through a fine, nylon sieve. Bottle and sterilize.

Note on bottling and sterilizing:
This sauce will keep in the fridge for about two weeks, so if only a small amount is being made, simply wash the jars or bottles well in hot water, dry them in a low oven and pour in the ketchup.

Tomatoes

Tomatoes may be grilled or fried for breakfast, either by themselves or with grated cheese on top. Hard Greek cheese, like feta, is good for this purpose. Tomatoes are one of the usual components of a mixed grill.

ŒUFS PROVENÇAL

Use very large tomatoes for this recipe. Slice off the tops and scoop out the centres of the tomatoes and reserve them for some other use. Break an egg into each tomato and grate a generous layer of cheese on top of each egg. Put the tomatoes on a greased dish and bake them in a hot oven for 10 minutes.

SCALLOPED TOMATOES

½ kg (1 lb) tomatoes
1 small onion
60 g (2 oz) butter
120 g (4 oz) brown breadcrumbs
120 g (4 oz) grated cheese
2 eggs, hard-boiled and chopped fine
1–2 teaspoons French mustard
1 teaspoon brown sugar
Salt and pepper

Chop the onion fine and simmer in the butter. Skin and chop the tomatoes and add them to the onion. Cook for 5 minutes with a seasoning of salt and pepper and a teaspoon of brown sugar. Add all the other ingredients, mix well and turn into greased scallop shells. Dot with butter and brown under a hot grill.

TOMATO SHAKE

200 ml (⅓ pint) tomato juice
1 dessertspoon lemon juice
A dash of Worcester sauce or Tabasco
2 tablespoons chopped parsley, spring onion or carrot
Salt and pepper

Put all the ingredients in a blender and liquidize. In the absence of a blender, leave out the chopped vegetables and shake the other ingredients in a milk bottle.

TOMATO KETCHUP

This is an excellent accompaniment to eggs and bacon or mixed grill. It is much more fruity and less sweet than commercial tomato ketchup. Make it especially at the end of the summer when tomatoes are often in glut. Use fresh savoury if possible — the summer or winter variety.

1 kg (2 lb) tomatoes
2 cloves garlic
1 medium-sized onion
2–3 tablespoons fresh savoury (half the amount if dried)
½ teaspoon paprika
1 teaspoon salt
60 g (2 oz) sugar
150 ml (¼ pint) vinegar

Peel and chop the tomatoes and simmer them with the garlic and onion in a covered pan until soft. Add the seasoning, sugar and vinegar and continue to cook for another 20 minutes. Adjust the seasoning to taste and either blend or sieve the liquid until it is of smooth consistency. Pour into warmed bottle using a funnel, and seal. If making larger quantities than those given in the recipe, sterilize the sauce bottles before storing.

GREEN-VEGETABLE SHAKE

Yoghurt and buttermilk combine well with the sharp, fresh taste of watercress, sorrel or spinach. Using either of these bases, roughly chop a small bunch of any of these greens (or a combination of them), add a little mint or spring onion if liked, season with pepper and salt and liquidize.

SWEETCORN GRIDDLE CAKES

120 g (4 oz) plain flour
120 g (4 oz) fresh or tinned sweetcorn
1 teaspoon salt
1 teaspoon baking powder
1 egg
Milk to mix

Mix the sweetcorn and egg together, then add the dry ingredients. Beat in enough milk to form a soft dropping consistency. Cook as in the previous recipe until the cakes are lightly browned on each side.

Freshly-picked sweetcorn grilled over charcoal also makes an excellent breakfast.

LAVERBREAD

The Welsh along with the Japanese, are unusual in having a seaweed as one of their traditional breakfast foods. Laver is a seaweed with thin, delicate, pale green leaves, which is commonly found around the British coast. These leaves are gathered and boiled down to make a brown, mushy substance known as laverbread. It may not look very appetizing in this form (this is how it is sold), but do not be put off by appearances.

To cook the laverbread, have ready a bowl of fine oatmeal and drop the seaweed into it, a tablespoon at a time. Coat it all over with oatmeal and fry as small cakes in a pan of hot bacon fat or oil. Serve hot, traditionally with bacon.

Vegetable Breakfasts in Japan, the Middle East and India

MISO SOUP WITH SEAWEED AND VEGETABLES

— a traditional Japanese breakfast.
Miso, the product of the fermented soya bean, is an extremely sustaining, high-protein food which therefore makes an excellent breakfast. It is quickly made by adding a dessertspoon of miso to a large breakfast cup of boiling water. Add a few strips of carrot, celery or spring onion, or of dried seaweed, and it is ready to drink.

EGYPTIAN BEANS

240 g (8 oz) haricot beans
240 g (8 oz) tomatoes
2 onions
4 cloves garlic
2 tablespoons chopped parsley
1 tablespoon chopped basil
Salt and pepper

Soak the beans in water overnight. Simmer for about one hour until tender. Fry the onions and garlic, then add the chopped tomatoes. Allow to simmer for 20 minutes and season with the chopped parsley, basil, salt and pepper. Add the beans to the sauce and serve.

Apparently the Israeli army took a fancy to this traditional Egyptian breakfast when they were occupying part of Egypt and adopted it as standard army fare.

FRIED AUBERGINES

Slice the aubergines and sprinkle well with salt. Leave, pressed by a heavy plate, for half an hour so that the bitter juices are extracted. Rinse off the salt and dry with a paper towel. Fry the aubergines in hot oil. They may be served with seasoned yoghurt.

Salads of green peppers, cucumber or tomatoes are often eaten at breakfast time in the Middle East, either with a yoghurt dressing or one of oil and vinegar.

ISRAELI KIBBUTZ BREAKFAST

When I worked on an Israeli kibbutz, breakfast was eaten around eight o'clock in the morning — about three hours after work had begun. Thus appetites were hearty and breakfasts substantial. I remember the trolleys being wheeled round laden with vegetable salads, curd cheeses and yoghurt, cold blancmange-like puddings and bread and matzos. Since our kibbutz specialized in fruit-growing, there was no absence of delicious peaches which were either too ripe or too large to be sent on.

The idea of eating raw vegetables for breakfast is now popular all over Israel. Even the best hotels will offer a vegetable breakfast. A selection of conveniently chopped vegetables — tomatoes, aubergines, peppers, celery, carrots, radishes, cucumber, etc. — are served with a bowl of dressing which is used as a dip. The dressing may be made with curd cheese or yogurt as well as oil and vinegar. This breakfast is ideal for a hot climate, being light as well as tasty and nutritious.

VEGETABLE-STUFFED PARATHAS

Parathas are similar to chapatis but are made with extra ghee or oil. They are often eaten for breakfast in India, stuffed with a spicy potato mixture — an excellent combination and not at all heavy as one might expect. The best accompaniment to this dish is cold yoghurt mixed with a little salt, pepper and chives.

PARATHAS

To make about eight:

180 g (6 oz) wholewheat flour
90 g (3 oz) plain flour
½ teaspoon salt
8 tablespoons ghee or oil (including that needed for frying)
200 ml (⅓ pint) water

Mix the flours with the salt and add the water plus two tablespoons of oil. Make a dough and knead for a few minutes. Leave in a covered bowl for half an hour or more. Roll out the dough to a thickness of about ½ inch and brush with oil. Roll up the dough, swiss-roll fashion and divide into eight pieces. Put on a skillet or thick pan to heat. On a well-floured board, roll out the parathas into circles, as thinly as possible. Spread one paratha with some of the vegetable mixture then place another one on the top, sealing the edges with thumb and fore-finger. Brush the upper side with oil and grease the pan. Cook for 2 minutes on each side.

101

PARATHAS — VEGETABLE FILLING

This should be prepared while the paratha dough is proving:

½ kg (1 lb) potatoes
2 medium onions
4–5 cloves of garlic
2 teaspoons grated ginger
2 teaspoons salt
2 teaspoons lemon juice
Salt/pepper, paprika, cumin, turmeric, to taste.

Boil and mash potatoes, chop and fry the onions, garlic and ginger in ghee or oil and mash with the potatoes, season with salt and pepper, lemon juice and spices. Fresh peas and mint may also be added with advantage.

Fish Breakfasts

"First of all they had a loaf of bread in trenchers, two manchets, a quart of beer and a quart of wine" then "two pieces of salt fish, six baconed herrings, four white herrings and a dish of sprats."

Breakfast of *My Lord and Lady Northumberland Household Book*,
1512

"A man of taste is seen at once in the array of his breakfast table . . . chocolate, coffee, tea, cream, eggs, ham, tongue, fowl, all these are good. . . . But the touchstone is fish . . . your country is pre-eminent in the glory of its fish for breakfast."

Thomas Love Peacock, *Headlong Hall*

One of my best breakfast memories comes from Morocco where I used to stay in a fishing village on the Mediterranean coast. Every night when the weather was favourable, the large, high-prowed boats would row out to sea with a bright lamp burning over the stern to attract the fish. In the morning they would sell their catch on the beach and we would buy sardines, take them straight home and grill them over charcoal to eat for breakfast. The custom of eating fish for breakfast in Britain must have originated with people who lived around the coast sampling the night's catch in the same way.

Of all the fish caught around the British coasts, none has been more important to the national sustenance than the herring. The herring fisheries date back a thousand years and all through the Middle Ages the herring, heavily salted and thus known as a "red herring", was a cheap and valuable source of protein. Thomas Nashe wrote in the sixteenth century: "A red herring is a wholesome thing on a frosty morning; it is a most precious fish merchandise because it can be carried all across Europe . . . the poorer sort make it three parts of their sustenance. . . . Nowhere are they better cured than at Yarmouth."

It was in and around Yarmouth that the bloater, then the kipper, were first cured, both much less salty and less harshly cured than the red herring and destined to become a favourite food for the Victorian breakfast table. Today the best kippers come from the Isle of Man and Craster in Northumberland where they are slowly smoked over oak fires in the traditional way.

Herrings

GRILLED HERRINGS

Many people think twice about eating herrings because of the numerous fine bones, which can be difficult to remove. If filleted in the following manner, however, most of the bones can be removed without too much difficulty:

Cut off the head and slit the fish all the way along the belly. Clean out the fish under the tap and remove the roe, if any, to cook separately. Then put the fish, back uppermost, on to a board and press down firmly along the backbone. Turn it over and it should be quite easy to pull out the backbone with most of the smaller bones attached.

Brush the outside of the fish with a little oil (not much because they are very oily fish) and put them under a hot grill to cook for three to five minutes on each side, depending on their size.

Mustard is the traditional accompaniment to herrings; or mustard butter, which is easily made by combining three tablespoons of butter with one tablespoon of made mustard.

HERRINGS FRIED IN OATMEAL

Clean and fillet the herrings. Season some medium oatmeal with a little salt. Coat the herrings well with oatmeal and fry in hot bacon fat or oil for three or four minutes on each side. Serve with lemon wedges and/or mustard butter.

SOFT HERRING ROE

Finely chop a small onion and soften it in butter. Add the chopped roes and fry gently for 5 minutes. Stir in a little cream and serve. Alternatively, make a batter with egg, flour and milk (see pancake section). Dip the roes in the batter and cook like fritters. Serve with lemon juice and pepper.

POTTED HERRINGS

This is a good spread for breakfast toast. It may of course be made at any time and stored in the fridge.

Clean and fillet the herrings and grill them. Remove the skin and any remaining bones (it will not matter if a few very fine ones are left in). Mash up the fish with an equal quantity of butter. Press into a bowl and cover with clarified butter.

Potted meats and fish are traditionally covered with clarified butter to exclude the air and thus help with preservation. If the spread is to be consumed quickly, it is not necessary to cover it with butter, but it makes a good finish to do so.

To clarify the butter: melt 500 g (1 lb) butter on a very low heat for one hour. Skim off the clear butter and leave the milky residue at the bottom of the pan. Wet some muslin and fold three or four times. Strain the clear butter through the muslin. Store in the fridge for future use.

Cod

COD'S ROE

Theodora FitzGibbon quotes the following recipe in *A Taste of Ireland*. It is a traditional Irish breakfast dish.

240 g (½ lb) cod's roe (cooked but not smoked)
240 g (½ lb) breadcrumbs
2 eggs
3 tablespoons cream
Juice of half a lemon
1 tablespoon parsley
Salt and pepper
Pinch of mace

"Mash the cod's roe. Beat the egg yolks with the cream. Combine all the ingredients together, except the egg whites, which should be whipped up and folded in last of all. Put the mixture in small ovenproof dishes and bake in a hot oven for 15 minutes or until just brown on top."

SMOKED COD'S ROE PASTE

Combine the smoked roe with a little less than its weight in butter (i.e. 120 g/4 oz roe to 90 g 3 oz butter). Season with lemon juice and pepper. Cover with clarified butter. This is very good on toast with scrambled egg.

Kippers

Kippers may be cut up (and eaten without further cooking), grilled, jugged or simmered in water for a very few minutes.

To fillet a kipper, lay it on a board, back side up. Remove the skin, then, with the point of a knife, remove the exposed flesh from the bone, which should, with any luck, remain intact.

If the kipper is grilled, place it with the skin side nearest the heat.

JUGGED KIPPERS

Simply fill a jug with boiling water and put the kippers into it. Leave to stand for 5–10 minutes in a warm place. Mrs Beeton says this produces nice, plump kippers, but some people think it loses some of the flavour.

KIPPER CAKES

240 g (8 oz) cooked potatoes
240 g (8 oz) filleted kippers
2 teaspoons made mustard
1 egg
60 g (2 oz) Parmesan or other grated cheese
Flour for coating, seasoned with salt

Cook and fillet the kippers and mash them with potatoes. Combine with the beaten egg, mustard and cheese. Form the mixture into round cakes, about one inch thick, roll them in the seasoned flour and fry them in oil until brown on either side.

KIPPER RAMEKINS

240 g (8 oz) cooked and filleted kippers
2 egg yolks
2 tablespoons thick cream
1 teaspoon made mustard
Seasoning of salt and pepper

Flake the kipper and beat it with the other ingredients. Butter some small oven-proof dishes and fill them with the mixture. Bake in a hot oven for about 10 minutes.

KIPPER PASTE

1 pair of medium-sized kippers
180 g (6 oz) butter
2 teaspoons lemon juice
½ teaspoon cayenne pepper
Clarified butter

Fillet the kippers and pound them with the butter until a smooth paste is formed. Add the lemon juice and pepper. Press into a bowl and cover with clarified butter.

SMOKED HADDOCK

"We breakfasted at Cullen. They set down dried haddock, broiled. ... I ate one but Mr Johnson disliked their presence and had them removed."

(Boswell, *Tour of the Hebrides*).

The best smoked haddock nowadays is Finnan haddock, which owes its name to the village of Findon, near Aberdeen, where a specially good method of curing haddock was developed.

Finnan haddock is very good simmered in a little milk for about ten minutes and served with a poached egg on top. Or the following recipe is delicious and takes only a little longer:

½ kg (1 lb) smoked haddock
450 ml (¾ pint) milk
2 hard-boiled eggs
2 tablespoons Parmesan cheese
1 tablespoon flour
1 tablespoon butter
A little pepper

Poach the haddock in the milk and butter and hard-boil the eggs. When the fish is soft, take it out of the pan, fillet it and keep it aside in a warm place. Stir in the flour into the milk in which the haddock was cooked and add the mustard, pepper and grated cheese. Stir until the sauce is thick. Chop the hard-boiled eggs finely and add them to the sauce. Pour the sauce over the fish and serve.

KEDGEREE

The name derives from an Indian dish called "Khichri" which the

Victorians brought back to England and adapted as a recipe for breakfast. Eliza Acton gives a simple version:

"Mix together equal quantities of boiled rice and cooked fish (smoked haddock is the best). Stir over the heat with 60 g (2 oz) butter and a seasoning of cayenne. Add two beaten eggs and serve the dish when these are just set."

When there is rice left over from the previous night's supper, kedgeree is quickly prepared in the morning for breakfast.

Here is another tasty variation:

240 g (8 oz) cooked, flaked smoked haddock
240 g (8 oz) cooked rice
2 small onions
2 teaspoons turmeric
1 teaspoon curry powder
Juice of one lemon
120 g (4 oz) butter
2 hard-boiled eggs, chopped

Chop the onions finely and soften them in half the butter. Add the turmeric, curry powder and juice of the lemon. Fry gently for a couple of minutes. Stir in the fish and rice and the rest of the butter. Hard-boil the eggs. Keep the rice and fish mixture over a low heat for about 10 minutes, stirring occasionally. Finally, chop the hard-boiled eggs and mix them lightly with the rest of the ingredients. Mushroom ketchup is a good additional seasoning for kedgeree.

SMOKED-HADDOCK PUFFS

This is another smoked-haddock recipe of Victorian origin:

240 g (½ lb) smoked haddock
2 eggs
3 tablespoons milk
60 g (2 oz) flour
1 small onion
Salt and pepper

Chop an onion fine and fry until soft. Cook and flake the haddock. Mix these with the beaten eggs, flour and seasoning to form a stiff, batter-like consistency. Heat some oil in a pan and fry the mixture a spoonful at a time. Serve with lemon juice.

A Scottish breakfast speciality was to serve smoked haddock with slices of smoked ham.

Anchovies

These tiny fish make up in flavour what they lack in size. They are very good combined with butter, on toast and also with eggs.

ANCHOVY BUTTER

This is a simply-made spread – a home-made version of Gentleman's Relish and, incidentally, much cheaper. It can be made with tinned anchovies but is better with salted ones which can be obtained from some Italian food shops.

240 g (½ lb) salted anchovies
240 g (½ lb) unsalted butter
Juice of half a lemon
1 teaspoon paprika (optional)

Remove the bones from the anchovies and rinse off the excess salt under the tap. Chop them small and mash them well with a large fork. Cut up the butter, soft but not melted and add it to the anchovies. Combine well together until the butter is completely integrated with the fish. Press into a bowl and cover with clarified butter.

SCOTCH WOODCOCK

This recipe uses anchovy butter to delicious effect:

Make a rich scrambled egg, using cream rather than milk in the mixture. Toast some rounds of bread and spread generously with anchovy butter. Pile the scrambled egg mixture on top and serve.

TURKISH SPREAD

A good, strong Edwardian concoction.

4 hard-boiled eggs
Small tin of anchovies
120 g (4 oz) peeled shrimps
½ teaspoon cayenne pepper
Juice of half a lemon
120 g (4 oz) unsalted butter

Chop the eggs, anchovies and shrimps into very small pieces. Season and mash all the ingredients very well into the softened butter.

FRICASSEE OF ANCHOVIES AND EGGS

4 hard-boiled eggs
Small tin of anchovies
120 g (4 oz) mushrooms
2–3 tablespoons thick or sour cream

Chop the mushrooms and fry them in a little oil and butter. Chop the eggs and combine them with the mushrooms. Add the anchovies, then the cream. Stir over the heat for a couple of minutes. Serve with toast.

SUMMER BREAKFASTS

"In the summer, and when they are available, always have a vase of freshly gathered flowers on the breakfast table and, when convenient, a nicely arranged dish of fruit. When strawberries are in season, these are particularly refreshing, also grapes, even currants."

Mrs Beeton, *Household Management*

"The dairy was certainly worth looking at... — such coolness, such purity, such fresh fragrance of new-pressed cheese, of firm butter, of wooden vessels perpetually bathed in pure water; such soft colouring of red earthenware and creamy surfaces, brown wood and polished tin, grey limestones and rich orange-red rust on the iron weights and hooks and hinges."

George Eliot, *Adam Bede*

113

Dairy Produce

A VICTORIAN CHILD'S BREAKFAST

Boil one pint of milk with 30 g (1 oz) sugar. Cut crusts of bread into small pieces and put in a hot bowl. Put on top of the crusts two small pieces of butter, a grating of nutmeg and a pinch of cinnamon. Pour over the boiling milk and serve hot without stirring.

CURDS AND WHEY AND CROWDIE

When fresh, unpasteurized milk is left to stand, the curds (milk solids) separate naturally from the whey (the clear watery part of the milk). If you have access to some untreated milk, you can make curds and whey by leaving a pint of milk in a bowl in a warm place for a couple of days. The curds may be flavoured with sugar, vanilla and spices and eaten alone or with fruit. The whey, which used to be considered the most refreshing of summer drinks, may be drunk on its own or saved for bread-making.

In the Scottish Highlands, another separated-milk product, Crowdie, used to be made with fresh milk from the cow. To make Crowdie, add one teaspoon of rennet to three pints of unpasteurized milk. Leave to stand until the whey can be poured off, leaving the solid curds. Add salt to these curds and eat them with oatcakes.

YOGHURT

Yoghurt is very refreshing for breakfast in summer. The enzymes whch it contains have been proved of great nutritional benefit. Balkan people often live to a ripe old age, a fact which they sometimes ascribe to their high consumption of yoghurt.

Yoghurt is easy and economical to make at home, without any special equipment.

1¼ litre (2 pints) milk
3 tablespoons powdered milk
3 tablespoons ready-made yoghurt

The powdered milk is not absolutely necessary but it makes for a more solid texture. Combine the milk with the powdered milk and put them in a saucepan. Bring up to the boil, then allow to cool to finger temperature. Add the yoghurt and stir it in very well. Pour into a china bowl and leave to stand in a warm place for about twelve hours. The warmth needed for making yoghurt is about the same as that needed for rising bread. Thus it may be left in an airing cupboard, near a radiator or standing in a larger bowl containing hot water (which should be kept hot for the first few hours). When the yoghurt is thick, put it in the refrigerator and use as required.

The yoghurt may be flavoured with chopped or crushed fruit. Cream may be added for a "Greek" type yoghurt.

CAROB YOGHURT

To half a pint of yoghurt, add 1 tablespoon of carob powder, 60 g (2 oz) chopped roasted almonds, 3 tablespoons of thick cream and honey or sugar to taste.

LABAN

This is a simple curd cheese common to many countries but especially enjoyed in Arab countries at breakfast time:

To every pint of yoghurt add 1 teaspoon of salt. Put the yoghurt in a sieve lined with muslin and leave the whey to drain out overnight. In the morning, season the yoghurt with a little paprika and fresh chopped herbs and form into small ball shaped cheeses. In the Lebanon, these are rolled in a mixture of toasted sesame and dried thyme.

APPLE SNOW

1 kg (2 lb) cooking apples
30 g (1 oz) butter
90 g (3 oz) sugar or honey
200 ml (1/3) pint yoghurt
2 egg whites

Peel, chop and core the apples and cook them in butter with a very little water. Stir in the honey or sugar when the apples are soft and

116

fluffy. Remove from the heat and allow to cool. Meanwhile, beat the egg whites stiff. When the apples are cool, beat in the yoghurt and lastly fold in the egg whites. Chill in the refrigerator.

FRUIT FOOLS

These are usually made by beating up or blending the fruit with the cream. A less rich type of fool can be made by using more yoghurt than cream. Try one pound of chopped or stewed fruit to half a pint of yoghurt to two tablespoons of single cream. Add sugar or honey to taste.

LASSI

A favourite cool drink in India. Shake up equal quantities of yoghurt and water. Flavour with either salt or sugar.

COLD MILK PUDDINGS

In Greece, almost every café has a huge refrigerator in which they keep, among other things, small bowls of delicious, milky puddings. These are very good for breakfast on hot summer mornings. Assuming a good supply of small bowls, these puddings may be made in quantity and kept in the fridge until required.

CREMA

600 ml (1 pint) of milk
2 tablespoons cornflour
2 tablespoons vanilla sugar
1 lemon
A few drops of vanilla essence
A little ground cinnamon

Mix the cornflour into a paste with a little of the milk. Bring the milk to the boil with the sugar and a spot of vanilla essence. Pour the milk over the paste, stirring all the time. Return the mixture to the saucepan and stir over the heat for a further couple of minutes. Pour into small basins and sprinkle with a little ground cinnamon. Put a slice of lemon on top of each bowl.

117

GROUND RICE AND ALMOND PUDDING

4 tablespoons ground rice
2 tablespoons ground almonds
450 ml (¾ pint) milk
60 g (2 oz) sugar
Peel of an orange, grated
A small piece of vanilla
Ground cinnamon

Pour the milk into the bowl with the vanilla. Add the ground rice and let it soak for about 15 minutes. Place the bowl over a pan of boiling water. Add the sugar, ground almonds and grated orange peel, stirring continuously until thick. Take out vanilla and pour mixture into bowls to set. Sprinkle on a little cinnamon.

MILK SHAKES

These can be made with a base of milk, yoghurt or buttermilk, or any combination of the same.

Strawberries, bananas, raspberries, blackberries, grapes, melons, pineapple, peaches and apricots are some of the many fruits which can be used in milk shakes. Use 120–250 g (4–8 oz) of fruit per 600 ml (1 pint) of milk and sweeten to taste. An egg yolk can also be included for extra sustenance. The white may be whipped up with some sugar and floated on the top of the liquid.

Milk shakes are best made in a blender but can also be made without. Crush the fruit thoroughly with a fork and add the milk. Finish by whisking the mixture with an egg whisk.

CREAMS AND CHEESES

In former times, every farmer's wife had her own way of making cream and curd cheese. In France there are still hundreds of regional variations. The simplest way of making a soft cheese, is to put some yoghurt in a muslin bag of two or three thicknesses. Suspend it over a bowl and leave overnight. In the morning the curds should be left in the bag and the liquid whey drained into the bowl. Take the curds out of the bag, make into a cheese shape and season with salt.

BANANA AND CREAM CHEESE: Mash 4 bananas with the juice of an orange. Beat in 180 g (6 oz) cream cheese with sugar or honey to taste. Eat with oatcakes or scones.

RICOTTA: a type of Italian curd cheese. This goes well with fresh soft fruits such as peaches or strawberries.

SOUR CREAM: try black cherries, when they are in season, with sour cream. This is a Russian favourite.

CHEESECAKE

This cheesecake should be left overnight to set in a freezer or the freezing compartment of a refrigerator.

240 g (8 oz) curd cheese
2 eggs
90 g (3 oz) castor sugar
Peel and juice of a lemon
180 g (6 oz) digestive biscuits, crushed fine
120 g (4 oz) butter

Crush the biscuits with the end of a rolling-pin or pestle. Mix them with the melted butter. Press the resulting mixture firmly into a shallow cake tin 8 or 9 inches across. Beat two separated egg yolks with the sugar and the juice and peel of a lemon in a china basin. Place this over a saucepan of boiling water and stir continuously until the mixture thickens (about 10 minutes). Remove from the heat and beat in the curd cheese (preferably the smooth variety). In a separate bowl, beat the egg whites stiffly and fold them lightly into the mixture. Pour over the biscuit crust and freeze overnight.

Fruit

FRESH FRUIT SALAD

Any combination of the following fruits may be used:

Chopped apples, bananas, grapes (halved with the pips removed), peaches, melons, pineapple, plums, pears, oranges, mangoes, cherries, strawberries, raspberries, blackberries, red- and black-currants (the list is not exhaustive).

Prepare the fruit and chop it up. Squeeze over it some lemon juice and some sugar to taste (this will draw the juices a little). Leave the bowl of fruit in the fridge and use it as required. You can also add to the bowl as you go along. Many of these fruits are available all the year, but don't miss the soft summer fruits which often have only short seasons.

DRIED-FRUIT SALAD

This is good to make in winter when a good variety of fresh fruit may be more difficult to obtain. Dried apricots, pears, apples, figs, dates, prunes, raisins and sultanas may be used alone or in combination with fresh fruit.

This is a recipe for a dried-fruit salad given by Claudia Roden in *Middle Eastern Cookery*:

½ **kg (1 lb) dried apricots**
240 g (8 oz) prunes
120 g (4 oz) raisins
120 g (4 oz) blanched almond halves
60 g (2 oz) pistachio nuts or pine nuts
120 g (4 oz) sugar
1 tablespoon rosewater
1 tablespoon orange-flower water

"Wash the fruit if necessary and put into a large bowl. Mix with the nuts and cover with water. Add sugar to taste and sprinkle with rose and orange-flower water. Let the fruit soak at least 48 hours. The syrup becomes rich with the juices of the fruit and acquires a beautiful golden colour."

120

CITRUS FRUIT GRILL

Peel and cut into segments a grapefruit and two oranges. Put them in a heat-proof dish and cover with brown sugar. Put the dish under a hot grill for a few minutes until the sugar melts. This is good with cold yoghurt.

TROPICAL FRUIT SALAD

For a special breakfast occasion.

Scoop out the inside of a pineapple or melon. Mix the fruit of one of these with chopped bananas and mangoes. Return the fruit to the shell and squeeze over the juice of a lemon and an orange. Chill.

COCONUT SALAD

Chop four bananas and four sweet oranges and a pineapple into slices. Arrange them in layers with a generous sprinkling of grated coconut and a little sugar on each layer. Chill overnight.

Toasted, slivered almonds are a useful addition to most fruit salads. Broken walnuts combine well with chopped apples, bananas and oranges. Try also pine nuts, pistachios and cashew nuts in combination with different fruit.

COMPÔTE

The Victorians were fond of making fruit into a "compôte" by poaching it in syrup. To make the syrup, a quantity of sugar (about 240 g (½ lb) to a pint) is simmered in water for about 15 minutes. Skim all scum as it rises to the top of the pan. Leave for some hours before using it to poach the fruit.

If this sounds too sweet, simply chop the fruit and simmer it in water with a little lemon juice and sugar or honey to taste.

121

For a dried-fruit compôte: soak the fruit overnight with some cinnamon and other spices if liked. Next day, add lemon juice to taste and bring the liquid to the boil. Simmer until the fruit is soft.

FRUIT FLUMMERIES

Flummeries are old-fashioned English dishes, originally intended as after-dinner puddings, but served cold they make fresh-tasting and nourishing breakfasts. They are made from stewed fruit which is thickened with some kind of flour or grain.

GOOSEBERRY FLUMMERY

¾ kg (1½ lb) gooseberries
300 ml (½ pint) milk
2½ tablespoons semolina
120 g (4 oz) sugar

Stem and wash the gooseberries and simmer in a minimal amount of water until they are soft. Warm the milk and add the semolina, sprinkling it in a little at a time. Bring to the boil, stirring all the time, then lower the heat and simmer for a couple of minutes. Sieve the fruit and add it, together with the sugar, to the semolina mixture. Put in a bowl and chill until set.

Plums, apricots, rhubarb or blackberries can also be used to make a flummery.

For a flummery thickened with cornflour instead of semolina, blend 1½ tablespoons of cornflour with a little cold milk, stir it into the warmed milk and proceed as above.

GRAPE OR APPLE JUICE FLUMMERY

600 ml (1 pint) grape or apple juice
3 tablespoons semolina
2 tablespoons sugar
Juice of a lemon

If grapes are plentiful, wash 2 lb and put them in a blender. Liquidize and then pass through a sieve to separate the skins and the pips. Otherwise use prepared grape (or apple) juice. Warm the liquid in a saucepan and sprinkle in the semolina a little at a time, stirring. Add the sugar and bring to the boil. Lower the heat and allow to simmer for about 5 minutes, stirring all the time. Add the lemon juice and pour into individual bowls to set. This is good to eat with yoghurt or cream.

APPLES AND GROUND ALMONDS

1 kg (2 lb) cooking apples
150 g (5 oz) ground almonds
60 g (2 oz) butter
Sugar to taste

Peel and slice the apples and put them in a saucepan with very little water, the butter and the sugar. Cook over a medium heat until they are soft, then stir in the ground almonds. This may be eaten hot or chilled, perhaps with a little cream or yoghurt.

Tea and Coffee

"Tea tempers the spirit and harmonizes the mind . . . lightens and refreshes the body and clears the perceptive faculty."

Lu Yu, 7th century

"The drink which has come to supply the place of beer has, in general, been tea. It is notorious that tea has no *useful strength* in it; that it contains nothing nutritious; that it, besides being good for nothing, has *badness* in it, because it is well known to produce lack of sleep in many cases, and in all cases to shake and weaken the nerves."

William Cobbett, 19th century

Tea

Ever since 1660 when Samuel Pepys "sent for a cup of tea (a China drink which I never had before)", tea rapidly became an indispensable feature of the English diet and the English breakfast. By the beginning of the nineteenth century, much to the chagrin of William Cobbett, even poor farm labourers were buying tea to drink in the morning instead of the traditional ale — with which they had started their day for many centuries. "It is impossible to make a fire, boil water, make the tea, drink it, wash up the things, sweep the fireplace and put all to rights again, in less space of time than two hours . . . by the time that the clattering tea-tackle is out of the way, the morning is spoiled and any work that is to be done afterwards lags heavily along."

Britain is traditionally the largest tea consumer in the world (about 4 Kg (8 lb) per capita per annum at the moment). India is the largest producer, growing a thousand million pounds annually, of which it consumes half (figures to make Cobbett turn in his grave. He would no doubt ascribe all India's economic problems to excessive tea drinking!).

Assam produces a strong, fine-flavoured tea. Darjeeling is a less strong yet subtly flavoured tea. In Ceylon light-flavoured teas are grown, reddish or golden-coloured, which taste better drunk with lemon than milk.

China, where tea was "discovered", as legend has it when a few leaves from a tea-bush fell into the Emperor's pot of boiling water, used to be by far the largest tea-growing country. Formerly no less than eight thousand grades of tea were recognized by the Chinese tea merchants. Tea was highly valued as a mental and even spiritual stimulant. Monks in the monasteries of China and Tibet habitually drank tea to keep warm, no doubt, but also as an aid to meditation. In Japan too, the drinking of tea was raised to spiritual significance with the development of the tea ceremony. Today, the best known teas exported from China are Keemun, a black tea with a full and interesting taste (this was the original "English Breakfast Tea") and Lapsang Suchong, with its distinctive smoky taste. Japan exports green unfermented teas and Formosa (Taiwan) grows green "gunpowder" tea and semi-fermented Oolong.

TO MAKE A GOOD CUP OF TEA

First warm the teapot and put in a teaspoon of tea for each person who will be drinking (a large teaspoon if only for one person and small ones for a larger number of people). It is a good idea to warm the tea leaves while the kettle is boiling, then when the kettle is at a full boil, pour the water over the leaves. Do not stir the pot. (In the North of England, there is a saying that to stir the pot is to stir up strife, but at any rate it does not improve the brew.) Leave the tea to stand in a warm place from three to eight minutes; the larger the leaf, the longer it will take to extract the flavour. Sugar is not recommended by tea connoisseurs but a sweet, strong cup of tea can be a welcoming thing. The Russians used to drink their black tea through a sugar lump held between the teeth.

HERBAL AND FLAVOURED TEAS

Tea may have different flowers, leaves and spices mixed into the blend to give even more variety of taste. It was traditional to add rose petals to certain China teas. Bergamot is the "secret" ingredient of Earl Grey blend.

Many such teas are now on the market — orange flower, hibiscus flower, lemon, apricot, blackcurrant, mango — to name but a few. It is possible to make one's own blend at home.

Before the import of China tea, the word "tea" was applied to any infusion of herbs. Much has been written about herbal teas, it is enough to say here that the infusion time is rather longer than for ordinary tea (ten to fifteen minutes) and the usual proportions used are 30 g (1 oz) to 600 ml (1 pint) of liquid. Lemon, verbena, rosehip, peppermint, camomile and hibiscus all make pleasant teas for breakfast, with or without the addition of honey.

People who want a stimulating drink in the morning, other than tea or coffee, might enjoy maté the South American "yerba buena". This plant has a high caffeine content and is usually drunk with milk or lemon and sugar. In South America it is often drunk from a gourd through a special straw-cum-strainer, called a bombilla.

ICED TEA

Make a pot of Ceylon tea. Pour it into glasses over ice. Add sugar to taste and some garnish — sprigs of mint, slices of orange, lemon or cucumber.

MOROCCAN MINT TEA

Put one teaspoon of green, unfermented tea per person into the pot. (In Morocco quite ornate silver or metal teapots are generally used and the tea is poured into glasses instead of cups.) Wash about half a dozen good stems of mint (spearmint) and put them in the pot with a spoonful of sugar for each person, or to taste. Pour over the boiling water and leave to infuse for five minutes. Sometimes orange flower petals and a little lemon verbena are put in the glasses and the tea is poured over them.

SPICED TEA

Tea similar to this is sold on cold winter evenings in the streets of Athens.

Boil two or three cinnamon sticks in half a pint of water for five minutes. Put two good teaspoons of black tea into the teapot and pour on the boiling cinnamon water. Allow to infuse and serve with a stick of cinnamon and sugar.

TEA CAUDLE

Possets and caudles were popular in former times as sustaining liquid snacks on journeys, for supper and for breakfast. Here is a seventeenth-century recipe for "tea caudle":

"Combine one quart of strong tea with one pint of white wine and the yolk of four beaten eggs. Heat them all together with sugar and nutmeg."

129

GLASSES VERSUS CUPS

"Because of a custom peculiar to Russia . . . men drink tea from glasses while women use cups from China. Here is the legend which relates to this custom.

"The first tea cups were made in Cronstadt. Now it often happened in cafés that, as an economy measure, less tea was put in the teapot than should have been. So if there was a picture of Cronstadt in the bottom of the cup, which was too much visible because of the transparency of the liquid, the tea drinker would call the proprietor of the café, show him the bottom of the cup and say to him: 'You can see Cronstadt.' The café proprietor could not deny that one could see Cronstadt; and since, if the tea had been as strong as it should have been, the view of Cronstadt would have been obscured, he was caught in the very act of fraud. Realizing this, the shop-keeper had the idea of substituting glasses with transparent bases, for the cups in which one could see Cronstadt."

Dumas, *Grand Dictionnaire de cuisine*

Coffee

"Amidst all those stars there was but one which could make itself significant to us by conjuring up that aromatic bowl . . . the joy of living, I say, was summed up for me in the remembered sensation of that first burning, aromatic mouthful, that mixture of coffee, milk and bread, the daily gift at dawn"

(Antoine de Saint-Exupéry, *Wind, Sand and Stars*.

Who has not, on occasions, felt a similar longing for the steaming bowl of *café au lait*? Coffee first reached Europe from the Near East in the seventeenth century. Coffee houses, which had long existed in Arab countries, were opened up in large numbers and soon became the social centres of the age.

The coffee plant was originally a native of Ethiopia, whence it was taken to Yemen and became the most popular drink of the Arabs.

Today it is grown mostly in South and Central America and the West Indies, East Africa, Indonesia and India. Two main qualities of coffee are recognized, the Arabica (grown mostly, but not entirely, in South and Central America) and the Robusta. The Arabica is usually more lightly roasted than the less delicate Robusta. Of course, coffee is sold in a huge variety of blends and roasts and it is largely a matter of trial and error to find one's preference. French coffee often has chicory added to it and Viennese coffee has ground figs.

There are several methods of making good coffee:

1. *Espresso*. (Italian for "quickly".) This method requires an Espresso machine, which works by forcing steam through the ground coffee. It is reckoned to be a very efficient and economical method because the coffee does not brew too much and the amount of coffee needed is relatively little. Capuccino coffee is espresso with frothy milk on top, sometimes sprinkled with slivers of chocolate.

2. *Filter*. A good, inexpensive method because the filter and filter papers are cheap to buy. Also, as with espresso the coffee should be very finely ground, which means that less is used per cup.

3. *Cona*. The water is heated in a glass container and the steam rises into a connecting vessel, through the gallery containing the coffee. This method also makes good coffee but the glass containers are rather fragile.

4. *Percolator coffee*. This is not so popular now because the water passes through the coffee more than once and has a tendency to make it "stew". Stove-top percolators are attractive objects in the kitchen, though. The coffee should be medium-ground for use in a percolator.

CAFÉ AU LAIT

Make some quite strong coffee by one of the above methods. Add an equal quantity of boiling milk. *Café au lait* is best served in bowls or bowl-shaped cups.

Austrian breakfast coffee is served with whipped cream and a twist of orange peel.

131

MOCHA

A mixture of coffee and chocolate. Boil some milk and add two teaspoonfuls of drinking chocolate. Add an equal quantity of black coffee. Alternatively, melt some cooking chocolate, stir in some cream and add it to the black coffee.

TURKISH COFFEE

This is generally made in a long-handled jug called an *ibrik*. Turkish coffee is strong and very finely ground and is usually taken sweet or medium sweet, as without sugar it is very bitter.

For one person, take a small ibrik and put in one cup of water and one teaspoon of sugar. Bring the water to the boil and add one heaped teaspoon of coffee. Reheat to boiling two or three times, taking the pot off the heat between whiles to let the froth subside.

In the Middle East, this coffee is often flavoured with cardamon seeds: one seed may be dropped into the pot at the same time as the coffee.

ICED COFFEE

Prepare some strong coffee and pour it into tall glasses containing ice. Try equal quantities of coffee, milk and cream.

OTHER KINDS OF COFFEE

Decaffeinated coffee retains the flavour of the coffee without the stimulating effect of the caffeine.

Roasted, ground dandelion roots, prepared like coffee, make a pleasant drink which has the added benefit of being good for the liver.

In war-time and other times of emergency, quite awful coffee has been prepared from ground, roasted acorns, but it is not recommended.

132

MARMALADES AND JAMS

The Dairymaid
Said "Fancy!"
And went to
Her Majesty.
She curtsied to the Queen, and
She turned a little red:
"Excuse me,
Your Majesty,
For taking
The liberty,
But marmalade is tasty, if
It's very
Thickly
Spread."

A.A. Milne, "The King's Breakfast"

The original marmalade was not made for spreading. It was a solid concoction of quinces, spices, honey and wine ("marmelo" is Portuguese for quince) rather like membrillo, a quince paste which is still made in Spain. The first marmalade such as we know was probably made by one James Keiller. This Scottish merchant had been rashly tempted to buy up a whole cargo of bitter oranges from a foundered Spanish ship. He was afterwards at a loss to know what to do with them, until his wife had the idea, so the story goes, of boiling them up with sugar to make a preserve. Marmalade remained a Scottish speciality until the mid-nineteenth century, when Mrs Cooper began to make her "Oxford" marmalade. Soon marmalade became a popular addition to the Victorian breakfast table.

Notes on making Marmalade and Jam

1. Since citrus fruit is so often heavily sprayed and treated for storage, give the skins a good scrub in hot water before using the peel.

2. The pith and pips of various fruits often have a high pectin content, therefore they are separated from the rest of the fruit, tied up in a muslin bag and boiled with the jam or marmalade to improve the setting quality.

3. There are different ways of testing to ensure that the preserve has been boiled for long enough and will set when cool. The usual method is to take out a spoonful and put it onto a cold saucer. If this forms a skin after a couple of minutes then the jam or marmalade has probably been cooked enough. If, during the course of the cooking, the mixture begins to turn brown, take it off immediately, as the sugar is beginning to caramelize. If in doubt, it is better to under-cook than over-cook because it is always possible to re-boil a batch which has not set properly.

4. Wash and rinse, very thoroughly, the jars to be used for the preserves. Set the oven at 150°–200° F (Gas mark ¼–½) and place the jars on the oven shelves. leave them there for about half an hour. If you do this while the preserve is cooking, they should be ready to take out, hot and dry, by the time they are required. Pour the preserve straight into jars and cover with a circle of greased paper.

The cellophane tops, secured by an elastic band, can be put on immediately, or when the jam is completely cold.

5. Store marmalade and jam in a cool dark place, if possible.

6. The pressure cooker: preserves can be made in a pressure cooker much more quickly and with no detriment to the ingredients. Pressure cookers are generally accompanied by instructions for making preserves. The soaking and simmering of the fruit is replaced by less than half an hour's cooking in the pressure cooker. The lid is then removed and the usual method followed.

7. Bottled pectin: the large amount of sugar required in most marmalade and jam is unappealing to some people. The sugar serves as a setting and preserving agent but it is possible to decrease the amount by using bottled pectin to set the preserve and keeping the resulting product in the refrigerator. The pectin is added last, after the mixture has been removed from the heat. Different fruits need different amounts of pectin; a rough average is half a bottle of pectin to 1 kg (2 lb) of fruit.

SEVILLE ORANGE MARMALADE

These bitter oranges are reckoned to be the best for making marmalade. They can usually be bought in England in late January and February.

1½ kg (3 lb) Seville oranges
3 kg (6 lb) sugar
2 large lemons
2½ litres (4 pints) water

Scrub the skins of the oranges. Peel them and remove the pips and the central pith. Chop the fruit roughly and the peel either finely or coarsely, depending if thin or thick-cut marmalade is required. Put the peel and fruit in a large bowl and cover with four pints of water. Put the pips and pith in a muslin bag and add to the bowl. Leave to stand overnight, then, next day, pour the whole contents of the bowl into a preserving pan. Simmer for one and a half to two hours, until the peel is tender and the water reduced to about half. Take out the muslin bag and add the warmed sugar. Stir until it is dissolved. Bring the mixture to the boil and keep it at a full "rolling boil" for about ten minutes. Test for setting and if it is ready, take off the heat and allow to cool for a few minutes before pouring into the warmed jars. Cover and seal.

THREE-FRUIT MARMALADE

When Seville oranges are out of season, marmalade may be made with a combination of sweet oranges, grapefruit and lemons.

1½ kg (3 lb) fruit, made up as follows:
1 grapefruit, 2 large sweet oranges and 4 lemons
3 kg (6 lb) sugar
2½ litres (4 pints) water

Scrub and chop the fruit. Reserve pith and pips in a muslin bag. Put everything into a large bowl and cover with four pints of water. Leave to soak overnight. Next day, pour the contents of the bowl into a preserving pan and bring to the boil. Reduce the temperature and simmer slowly until the peel is soft (about 45 mins.). Take out the muslin bag and add the warmed sugar. Stir until it is completely dissolved. Bring the mixture to the boil and let it boil for about 10 minutes, then test for setting. If it is not ready, continue to boil. When setting point is reached, leave to cool for a few minutes then bottle and cover in the usual way.

For four-fruit marmalade, make up 1½ kg (3 lb) of fruit with 1 grapefruit, 2 small oranges, 2 lemons and 2 cooking apples. Put the peel and pips of the apples in the muslin bag to increase the pectin content and proceed as above.

These marmalades may be flavoured with coriander or ginger if liked. Crush two tablespoons of coriander or 30 g (1 oz) of ginger and put in the muslin bag with pith and pips, remove before the sugar is added.

THREE-DAY MARMALADE

This is the surest and best marmalade recipe I have discovered. The long soaking period means that only a short boil is required for setting, thus preserving most of the flavour of the fruit. The idea comes from Jane Grigson (*Fruit Book*) who in turn was given the recipe, she says, at St Benoît-sur-Loire in France.

2 kg (4 lb) oranges (or mixture of citrus fruits)
1¾ kg (3½ lb) sugar
900 ml (1½ pints) water

Chop up the fruit, making sure that the peel is cut fine or coarse as required. Cover with 900 ml (1½ pints) of water and leave to soak for one day. Then, in a preserving pan, slowly bring the fruit and water to simmering point. Allow to simmer gently for an hour and then leave to soak for a further 24 hours. Heat the sugar while again bringing the fruit and water to the boil. Add the sugar and allow to boil rapidly until setting point is reached. Bottle in the usual way.

LIME MARMALADE

¾ kg (1½ lb) of limes
1¼ kg (2½ lb) sugar
2 litres (3 pints) water

Scrub the fruit in hot water and cut them in half. Squeeze the juice into a basin and keep it on one side. Pare the skin finely (you will need a very sharp knife because it is harder than orange or lemon peel) and cover with 2 litres (3 pints) of water. Leave to soak for some hours. Pour the water and peel into a preserving pan and simmer for about an hour or until the peel is soft and the water is reduced by half. Pour in the juice and the warmed sugar. Bring slowly to the boil then boil rapidly until setting point is reached. Bottle and cover.

This recipe may also be made using half lemons and half limes.

RHUBARB MARMALADE

1 kg (2 lb) rhubarb
1 kg (2 lb) sugar
2 oranges
2 lemons
1 teaspoon ground ginger
1 teaspoon ground cinnamon

Wash and peel 1 kg (2 lb) of rhubarb and cut into pieces about 1 inch long. Chop the fruit of two oranges and two lemons and pare the skins quite finely. Add the fruit and chopped peel to the rhubarb. Cover with sugar and leave overnight or all day. Then pour the fruit and dissolved sugar into a pan and place over a low heat. Add the ground ginger and cinnamon. Bring very slowly to the boil, taking about half an hour. When boiling point is reached, boil rapidly for about ten minutes, or until setting point is reached. Leave to cool slightly, then pour into jars and cover. This jam sets easily, so be careful not to over-boil. Test for setting after 6 or 7 minutes.

LEMON AND APPLE MARMALADE

4 lemons
1½ kg (3 lb) cooking apples
1½ kg (3 lb) sugar
1½ litres (2½ pints) water
A few cloves (optional)

Squeeze the juice from the lemons with a squeezer and reserve it in a basin. Chop the peel quite finely and put it in a bowl. If there are a lot of pips, put them in a muslin bag and into the basin. Pour over the water and leave to stand overnight. Next day, pour the contents of the bowl into a preserving pan and bring to the boil. Allow to simmer for about an hour. Meanwhile, peel and chop 1½ kg (3 lb) of cooking apples and add them to the pan when the lemon peel is already quite soft. Simmer until the apples are tender and add a few cloves for flavouring if liked. Take out the muslin bag and add the warmed sugar, stirring. Bring the mixture to the boil and continue to boil and stir until setting point is reached. Cool slightly and bottle in the usual way.

QUINCE MARMALADE

5 ¾ kg (1½ lb) quinces
½ kg (1 lb) sugar
450 ml (¾ pint) water

Peel and core the quinces and cut them up. Cover with a small amount of water and simmer until soft. Dissolve the sugar in half a pint of water and add the fruit to it. Bring slowly to the boil and stir continuously until the mixture thickens. Cover and bottle in the usual way.

PINEAPPLE MARMALADE

1 pineapple
3 sweet oranges
3 lemons
1 cooking apple
1 kg (2 lb) sugar
300 ml (½ pint) water

Squeeze the juice from the oranges and lemons, pare the skins and reserve the pith and the pips. Simmer the peel in a pint of water for about an hour and a half. Put the pith and pips in a muslin bag and place in the pan. Chop up the pineapple very small (the fibres of the pineapple do not break down during cooking). Also peel and chop the apple. Add these to the pan and continue to simmer for another half an hour. Add 1 kg (2 lb) of warmed sugar and bring to the boil. Stir and boil until setting point is reached. Slightly cool and bottle.

Jams

GOOSEBERRY JAM

1¼ kg (2½ lb) gooseberries
600 ml (1 pint) water
1½ kg (3 lb) sugar

Top and tail the gooseberries and wash them. Put them in a preserving pan with the water and simmer gently until soft (about 45 minutes). Warm the sugar and add it to the gooseberries, stirring until it has completely dissolved. Bring the mixture to the boil and boil rapidly for ten minutes. Take off the scum as it rises to the surface of the boiling jam. Test for setting after 10 minutes, if ready, pour the jam into clean, warmed jars and bottle in the usual way.

CHERRY JAM

1 kg (2 lb) cherries
½ kg (1 lb) sugar
Juice of 2 lemons

Wash and stone the cherries. Crack a few kernels and put them in with the fruit. Put into a bowl and cover with the lemon juice and sugar. Leave to stand for a few hours. Transfer to a preserving pan and bring the mixture to the boil as slowly as possible. When boiling point is reached, turn up the heat and boil rapidly, stirring, for about ten minutes. Test for setting (this jam will not set very hard) and if ready, cool a little and bottle. If making a large batch of cherry jam which will be kept for a long period, use more sugar — about 360 g (12 oz) to each 500 g (1 lb) of cherries.

MARROW JAM

George Bernard Shaw used to have marrow jam for breakfast.

2 kg (4 lb) marrow
2 kg (4 lb) sugar
30 g (1 oz) root ginger
Rind and juice of 3 lemons
30 g (1 oz) stem ginger

Peel the marrow and remove the seeds. Dice the flesh into half-inch cubes and put them into a basin along with the chopped stem ginger. Cover with 500 g (1 lb) of sugar and leave overnight. Bruise the root ginger to release the flavour and tie it, together with the lemon rind, in a muslin bag. Put the marrow and ginger, together with the lemon juice, in a pan, tie the muslin bag to the handle and allow the contents to dip beneath the surface of the liquid. Simmer for half an hour. Add the rest of the warmed sugar and bring slowly to the boil. Boil rapidly until setting point is reached, by which time the liquid should be transparent. Bottle and cover in the usual way.

GRAPE AND APPLE JAM

1 kg (2 lb) grapes
½ kg (1 lb) cooking apples
2 lemons
¾ kg (1½ lb) sugar

Wash the grapes and take out the pips. Peel and core the apples and cut into slices. Squeeze the juice from the lemons and finely grate the peel. Simmer the fruit in a minimal amount of water for about an hour and a half. Add the warmed sugar and bring slowly to the boil. Boil rapidly until setting point is reached. Bottle and cover in the usual way.

TANGERINE JAM

This recipe is given by Claudia Roden in *Middle Eastern Cookery*.

1 kg (2 lb) tangerines
1 kg (2 lb) sugar

"Cut the tangerines in half and squeeze out the juice. Pour into a bowl and set aside. Remove the thin skins which separate the segments inside the peel. Then simmer the peel in water until soft, say seven to ten minutes. Drain well, cover with a fresh portion of cold water and soak for twelve hours or overnight, changing the water once or twice, if possible, to get rid of all the bitterness. Drain the peel and put it through the coarse blade of a mincer, or chop it roughly, using a mezzaluna chopper if you have one. Pour the reserved tangerine juice into a large saucepan. Add the sugar and the minced or chopped peel; simmer until the syrup is slightly thickened and the juice forms a firm jelly when a drop is left on a cold plate. It takes fifteen to thirty minutes. Let the jam cool slightly, then pour it into clean, warmed jars and seal tightly."

RASPBERRY AND APRICOT JAM

250 g (½ lb) raspberries
1¼ kg (1½ lb) apricots
1¼ kg (1½ lb) sugar
Juice of a lemon

Wash and mash the raspberries. Wash the apricots and take out the stones. Put the fruit in a preserving pan with the juice of the lemon and simmer without adding any water, for about an hour. Add the warmed sugar, without raising the temperature and stir until it is dissolved. Bring slowly to the boil and continue to boil for 10 to 15 minutes. Test for setting and, if ready, allow to cool slightly, bottle and cover.

RHUBARB AND GINGER JAM

1 kg (2 lb) rhubarb
1 kg (2 lb) sugar
15 g (½ oz) root ginger
2 lemons

Peel and chop the rhubarb into pieces about 1 inch long. Put it in a bowl with the lemon juice and cover with sugar. Leave to stand overnight. Pour the contents of the bowl into a pan and leave to simmer on a very low heat for an hour. The ginger should be bruised, tied in a muslin bag and allowed to simmer with the fruit. Raise the heat and bring to the boil. Remove the ginger and boil rapidly until setting point is reached. Test after 5 minutes as this jam is quick to set. Put into jars and cover.

Instead of ginger, this jam may be flavoured with almonds. Follow the above method (omitting the ginger) and when the jam has finished boiling, add 60 g (2 oz) of blanched, split almonds.

REDCURRANT JELLY

This recipe may also be used for making bramble and cranberry jelly.

2½ kg (5 lb) redcurrants
Sugar

Remove the leaves and all but the smallest stems from the fruit. Wash and slightly mash the fruit before putting into the preserving pan. Simmer the fruit slowly, without adding any water, for about forty-five minutes. Pulp the fruit with a potato masher or some other suitable implement and pour it into a large muslin bag. Suspend this over a bowl and allow the juice to drip through overnight. Next day, measure the juice and for every 600 ml (1 pint) of juice, add 750 g (1¼ lb) of sugar. Bring the fruit juice and the sugar to the boil, stirring constantly. Boil for about a minute only. Skim off the scum and pour the jelly into warmed jars. Cover and bottle.

RASPBERRY PRESERVE

½ kg (1 lb) raspberries
360 g (12 oz) castor sugar

This jam involves almost no work at all. It does not set quite so much as boiled jam, but the fruit flavour is unimpaired.

Put the fruit and the sugar in two separate bowls, covering the top of the fruit bowl with foil. Preheat the oven to 250° F (130° C, Gas mark ¾) and put the two bowls in the oven for half an hour. Take them out at the end of the time and mix the contents together. Put into jars, cover and seal. This should keep in a cool place for some months.

APPLE CONSERVE

½ kg (1 lb) cooking apples
300 g (10 oz) castor sugar
2 lemons
1 cinnamon stick

This is a non-setting preserve; the apple slices remain whole in the thick syrup. It makes a good "sauce" for pancakes and waffles and it is also good with cereal flakes and yoghurt.

Peel and core the apples and cut them in slices. Put them into a china jug or, ideally, a stone jar. Add the sugar, cinnamon stick, lemon juice and finely grated lemon rind. Stand the jug or jar in a saucepan of boiling water and shake from time to time. After about 40 minutes, the mixture should be clear and the apples soft. Put into jars and cover.

BANANA SPREAD

1 kg (2 lb) bananas
150 ml (¼ pint) lime juice (or lemon, if lime is not obtainable)
240 g (8 oz) sugar

This is a West Indian recipe and one which will probably be popular with children. Mash the bananas well and mix in the lime juice and sugar. Put the mixture into a stone jar or oven-proof vessel and cover the top with foil. Pre-heat the oven to 200° F (100° C, Gas mark ¼) and place the jar on the middle shelf. Shake well from time to time to prevent the mixture separating. After about one hour it will be ready. Put into jars and cover. Store in the refrigerator or a cold place.

Fruit Cheeses

Use a thick china bowl or jug set over, or inside, a saucepan of boiling water.

LEMON CHEESE

2 large lemons or 3 small ones
180 g (6 oz) sugar
3 eggs

144

Squeeze the juice of the lemons into a basin. Finely grate the peel of one and add it to the juice. Beat the eggs together in another bowl. Combine the lemon, eggs and sugar in the basin and place over a saucepan of boiling water. Stir constantly until thick (10–15 minutes) then pour into a clean warm jar. Store in the refrigerator, but it will probably be eaten too quickly for storage to be much of a problem.

My Welsh grandmother used to make this delicious spread in a special jug kept for the purpose. It is infinitely nicer than commercial lemon curd.

APRICOT CHEESE

1¼ kg (1½ lb) apricots
240 g (8 oz) sugar
2 beaten eggs

Cut the apricots in half and remove the stones. Steam the fruit until it is soft, then rub through a sieve to remove the skins. Put the pulp in a basin, together with the sugar and the beaten eggs. Place the basin over a saucepan of boiling water and stir continuously until thick (10–15 minutes). Pour into clean, warmed jars. Crack a few of the apricot stones and put the kernels into the cheese to add extra flavour. Store in the refrigerator.

Apricot cheese can also be made in a similar manner using equal quantities of apricot pulp and sugar, plus the juice of a lemon. This will store out of the refrigerator but is rather sweet for my taste.

GOOSEBERRY CHEESE

½ kg (1 lb) gooseberries
2 beaten eggs
120 g (4 oz) sugar

Wash the gooseberries and simmer them in a very little water until tender. Rub them through a sieve. Put the fruit, sugar and well beaten eggs in a china bowl and set the bowl over a saucepan of boiling water. Stir constantly for about 10 minutes or until the mixture has become thick. Pour into a clean, warmed jar and allow to cool. Refrigerate or leave in a very cool place.

APPLE CHEESE

½ kg (1 lb) cooking apples
3 lemons
180 g (6 oz) castor sugar
2 eggs

Peel, core and slice the apples and simmer them with the juice of one lemon until soft. Mash them thoroughly and put in a basin with the sugar, juice and finely grated rind of two lemons. Mix in the two well beaten eggs and set the basin over a saucepan of boiling water. Stir until the curd thickens, which will take about 20 minutes. Put into a clean, warmed jar and cover. Refrigerate or store in a cold place.

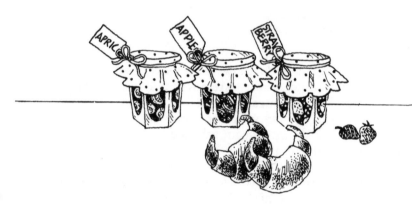

Festive Breakfasts

Most of the recipes in this chapter are associated with Easter. When Lent was strictly observed, Easter morning was celebrated with a huge feast, (as it still is in Russian and Greek Orthodox circles). All the foods which had been forbidden during Lent, like eggs, meat and cream would appear on the table in great profusion.

On Easter Saturday it used to be the custom in Russia for families to visit the cemetery and leave Kulich (Easter cake) and other food on the graves of their relatives. On Easter morning another large Kulich was taken to church to be blessed. This custom is still observed among believers.

In Greece, where Easter is still the most important festival of the year, Easter is heralded by the appearance in the baker's shops of large round or plaited loaves with a bright red egg embedded in their centre.

In England, we retain two reminders of the traditional Easter feast — the Easter egg and the hot cross bun. It is interesting to note that in the Middle Ages, all loaves were marked with a cross before they went into the oven, a custom that is now only retained for Good Friday.

147

Easter Breakfasts

KULICH

½ kg (1 lb) flour (plain white or half wholewheat and half white)
½ teaspoon salt
2 level teaspoons dried yeast (or 30 g/½ oz fresh)
150 g (5 oz) butter
120 g (4 oz) sugar
3 eggs
60 g (2 oz) raisins
60 g (2 oz) candied mixed peel
60 g (2 oz) chopped blanched almonds
1 level teaspoon ground cardamon
1 level teaspoon ground cinnamon
300 ml (½ pint) warm milk and water mixed

Sift the flour and the salt and dissolve the yeast in a little of the warmed water and sugar. Make a well in the centre of the flour and pour in the creamed yeast. Mix, then add the rest of the liquid. Mix well and knead and leave to rise in a warm place for an hour. Cream the butter, sugar and egg yolks. Combine with the raisins, candied peel and chopped almonds, cinnamon and cardamon. Add this mixture to the yeasted flour, working it in by hand. Beat the egg-whites stiff and fold them into the mixture. Put the dough into a greased tin (a tall cylindrical tin is traditional) and leave in a warm place until it is more than doubled in size. Bake at 375° F (190° C, Gas mark 5) for 50 minutes. For the glaze, boil together an equal amount of milk and sugar and brush it over the cake while it is still hot. Let the cake cool before taking it out of the tin and then turn it out onto a wire rack. The top of the cake may be decorated with blanched almond halves and glacé fruit.

PASHKA

Pashka (the Russian word for Easter) is made from cream, curd cheese, butter, eggs and sugar. It is traditionally made in a tall, pyramid-shaped mould, with crosses or XB "Christ is risen" engraved inside.

½ kg (1 lb) curd cheese
120 g (4 oz) double cream
60g (2 oz) butter (unsalted)
2 egg yolks
90 g (3 oz) sugar
Piece of vanilla pod
Peel of 2 oranges and 2 lemons
120 g (4 oz) blanched almonds

If the curd cheese is very moist, put it into a muslin bag to drain overnight. Squeeze out as much moisture as possible (the cheese was usually pressed under a weight for this purpose). Put the cream and the vanilla pod into a saucepan and bring to the boil. Beat the butter with the sugar and the egg yolks until creamy. Add it to the cream and stir over a low heat until the mixture is thick. Take off the heat and beat in the cream cheese. Add the chopped almonds and peel. Form the mixture into a pyramid shape when it is cool. Chill in the refrigerator for a day if possible, not less than twelve hours. Decorate the finished mould with nuts and glacé fruit.

A much simplified and less rich version of this dish, perhaps more suitable for those who have not carried out a strict Lenten fast, can be made as follows:

Mix 240 g (½ lb) curd cheese with 240 g (½ lb) of cream cheese. Add 120 g (3 oz) sugar, the peel of 2 oranges and 2 lemons and 120 g (4 oz) chopped, blanched almonds. This is very good eaten with fresh fruit, especially pineapple, which is easily obtainable around Easter time.

HOT CROSS BUNS

This recipe makes 15-20 buns:

¾ kg (1½ lb) flour, half plain and half wholewheat
1 teaspoon salt
2 teaspoons dried yeast (or 30 g/½ oz fresh
120 g (4 oz) currants
90–120 g (3–4 oz) brown sugar
60 g (2 oz) mixed peel
120 g (4 oz) butter

3 teaspoons mixed spice, made up of:
1 teaspoon cinnamon, ½ teaspoon cardamon, ½ teaspoon allspice,
½ teaspoon coriander, ½ teaspoon nutmeg
450 ml (¾ pint) milk and water mixed

Cream the yeast in a little of the warmed water with the sugar. Add it to the sifted flour and salt. Mix, then pour in the rest of the liquid and mix again. Add the currants, peel, spice and sugar. Mix and knead well, then leave to rise in a warm place for about an hour, or until the dough has doubled in size. Melt the butter slowly until it is almost liquid and work it well into the dough. Knead for 5 minutes (do not skimp this as it helps the buns to rise into a good rounded shape.) Leave to rise for a further 30 minutes. Form the dough into buns and incise each one with a cross using the blunt side of the knife. Place on a greased baking tray and leave until roughly doubled in size, which should take about 20 minutes. Meanwhile preheat the oven to 400° F (200° C, Gas mark 6). When they are ready, put the buns in the oven and bake for 20 minutes.

EASTER BREAD

This is my own recipe for Easter bread which, because of the marzipan, bears some resemblance to Simnel cake, traditionally eaten in England around Easter time, and to German stollen bread. Stollen has a layer of marzipan running through the centre, but I prefer to break the marzipan up into small lumps so that you come across nuggets of sweetness in a not-so-sweet bread. It is good to be generous with the wheatgerm as this gives a good texture and counteracts the sogginess to which the fruit bread is prone.

600 g (20 oz) plain and wholewheat flour mixed
150 g (5 oz) wheatgerm
2 teaspoons salt
1 tablespoon dried yeast
2 dessertspoons black treacle
240 g (8 oz) raisins
180 g (6 oz) marzipan
180 g (6 oz) butter or margarine
2 heaped tablespoons brown sugar
180 g (6 oz) blanched almond halves
450 ml (¾ pint) water

Mix the flour, wheatgerm and salt together. Rub in 120 g (4 oz) butter or margarine. Cream the yeast with the black treacle in a little warm water. When it has dissolved, pour it into the flour mixture. Gradually add the rest of the liquid, stirring well. Add the raisins, brown sugar, marzipan pieces and blanched almond halves, reserving some of the latter for the top of the loaf. Mix and knead well. Work the remaining two ounces of butter into the dough. Leave to rise in a warm place for 1–2 hours, after which, knead again, then divide dough between two 500 g (1 lb) bread tins. Put the remaining almonds on top of the loaves and leave to rise again until the dough is nearly up to the top of the tins. Preheat the oven to 400° F (200° C, Gas mark 6). Cover the top of the loaves with foil and bake for 15 minutes at 400° F (200° C, Gas mark 6) and 25 minutes at 350° F (180° C, Gas mark 4). Remove the foil 10 minutes from the end of baking, so that the almonds will brown.

GREEK EASTER BREAD

360 g (12 oz) plain flour
360 g (12 oz) wholewheat flour
2 level teaspoons dried yeast (or 30 g/½ oz fresh)
1 beaten egg
60 g (2 oz) melted butter
90 g (3 oz) brown sugar
Rind of an orange and a lemon
1 level teaspoon cinnamon
1 level teaspoon allspice
¼ teaspoon nutmeg
300 ml (½ pint) milk to mix
1 hard-boiled egg, dyed red

Cream the yeast in a little warm water with one tablespoon of the sugar. Sift the flour with all the dry ingredients. Mix in the creamed yeast and, gradually, the rest of the liquid. Add the beaten egg. Knead thoroughly then leave to rise in a warm place for about 1½ hours. When the dough is well risen, knock it down and knead again. Divide it into three parts. Roll each part into a sausage shape about 18 inches long. Grease a baking tray and plait the three lengths of dough on the tray. Join one end of the plait to the other to form a circle. Leave to rise for another 30–45 minutes. Bake for 15 minutes at 400° F (200° C, Gas mark 6) and a further 30 minutes at 375° F (190° C, Gas mark 5). Boil an equal amount of milk and sugar for the glaze and brush this on as soon as the loaf comes out of the oven. Set the coloured egg in the middle of the loaf when it is cool.

At New Year, a similar spicy loaf is made in Greece called Vasilopita. The date of the New Year is marked out in almonds on the top of the loaf and a coin, which will bring good luck to the one who finds it, is hidden inside. This bread is traditionally cut just after midnight on New Year's Day.

Champagne Breakfast

Should I be able to afford the luxury of champagne for breakfast, I would choose to accompany it with one of my favourite foods — scallops, lightly grilled with a little cheese and pepper. Others might prefer oysters, smoked salmon, smoked eels or perhaps anchovies served on thin slices of toast.

Here are three savouries which might also go down well:

ANGELS ON HORSEBACK

Take an equal number of oysters and rashers of bacon. Wrap each oyster in a bacon rasher. Secure with a skewer and grill until the bacon is just crispy.

MUSHROOMS IN HEAVEN

Slowly fry two or three rashers of chopped bacon with a little butter. When they are nearly done, add 250 g (8 oz) of finely chopped mushrooms and a little minced garlic. Fry rapidly, stirring, for about 3 minutes, seasoning with salt and pepper. Add 4 tablespoons of champagne or white wine. Cook rapidly for 2 minutes until the liquid is reduced. Serve on thinly buttered toast.

HAM DIABOLO

Dice 250 g (8 oz) of good ham and put it in a pan with 90 g (3 oz) butter, 2 teaspoons French mustard, one saltspoon of paprika and a dash of chilli sauce. Cook for a few minutes, stirring. Add 2 tablespoons of cream, if liked, and serve with thin toast.

The best champagne should probably not be adulterated, but some people may like to make an American "Mimosa" by mixing equal parts champagne and orange juice.

Birthday breakfasts for children

Here are three suggestions which have proved popular with children of my acquaintance.

PETIT PAIN AU CHOCOLAT

This recipe can be partially prepared overnight.

360 g (12 oz) plain flour
120 g (4 oz) wheatgerm
1 teaspoon dried yeast (2 teaspoons fresh)
1 small teaspoon salt
120 g (4 oz) butter
75 g (2½ oz) sugar
210 g (7 oz) plain chocolate
300 ml (½ pint) water

Mix the flour with the wheatgerm and salt. Heat a little of the water and dissolve the yeast with one tablespoon of the sugar in it. Rub the

154

butter into the flour and add the rest of the sugar. When the yeast is creamed, pour it into the centre of the flour mixture. Mix in and slowly add the rest of the warmed water. Knead well and leave the dough in a polythene-covered bowl in a warm place, overnight. In the morning, knead for about 5 minutes, then divide the dough into about fifteen rolls. Insert an equal amount of chocolate into the centre of each. Leave to rise on a greased baking tray until the rolls are doubled in size (which should not take more than half an hour). Bake in a hot oven, 400° F (200° C, Gas mark 6) for 25 minutes.

DOUGHNUTS

These are infinitely better than the shop variety and the dough can also be prepared overnight.

270 g (9 oz) flour (half plain, half wholewheat)
90 g (3 oz) sugar
1 beaten egg
1 tablespoon melted butter
1 heaped teaspoon baking powder
½ teaspoon salt
Grating of nutmeg
280 ml (a little under ½ pint) milk
Oil for frying

Mix all the ingredients together except the flour. Gradually add in the latter, beating well. When all the flour has been added, the batter should be just firm enough to handle. Leave in a cool place for at least an hour (or overnight). On a very well floured board, press out the dough to a thickness of about half an inch. Cut into circles about 4 inches across and cut a hole about 1 inch across out of the centre of each doughnut. Heat 2–3 inches of oil in a (preferably high-sided) pan to about the temperature generally used for frying chips. Drop in the doughnuts three at a time and cook for about 2 minutes on each side, or until just brown.

YOGHURT ICE CREAM

150 ml (¼ pint) yoghurt
2 tablespoons castor sugar
150 ml (¼ pint) thick cream
3 tablespoons crushed soft fruit (strawberries, raspberries, peaches, etc.)

Beat the sugar and the soft fruit with the yoghurt. Whip up the cream and fold into the mixture. Spoon into a mould or small bowls and leave to set in the freezing compartment of the refrigerator for at least 3 hours.

For vanilla ice cream, leave a small stick of vanilla in the yoghurt for a few hours before making the ice cream.

CHRISTMAS BREAKFAST

PANNETONE

This yeasted cake made in Italy at Christmas time makes an excellent Christmas breakfast, being festive but not too rich.
Here is my version:

720 g (24 oz) flour (half plain, half wholewheat)
1 teaspoon dried yeast (2 teaspoons fresh)
120 g (4 oz) butter
120 g (4 oz) sugar
120 g (4 oz) candied orange and lemon peel
90 g (3 oz) glacé cherries
90 g (3 oz) raisins
1 small teaspoon cinnamon
Grating of nutmeg
300 ml (½ pint) milk
1 small teaspoon of salt

Heat the milk to boiling and melt the butter in the milk. Dissolve the yeast in a little warm water with one tablespoon of the sugar. When the milk is cool, add the yeast, the sugar, dried fruit and spices. Gradually beat in the mixed flours. Knead well when all the flour has been added. Leave in a bowl covered in polythene for about 3 hours to rise. Knead again and divide the dough into two loaves. Place on a greased oven tray and leave to rise in a warm place until doubled in size. Bake in a moderate oven, 375° F (190° C, Gas mark 5) for 40 minutes.

Index

157